Mozart
at **250**

1756–(1791)–2006

K1–K626

b. Jan 27,
1756
8 p.m.

d. Dec 5, 1791
12:55 a.m.

ROGER MUSKER

suggestion of Tourette's syndrome. p. 50

MUSKER, DENBY AND HIRTZEL

2006

" Mozart is too easy for children and too
difficult for adults". Alfred Brendel.
b. 1931, Moravia, Austria

For A.A.C.M. RWS

Great work has been carried out by Rosie Anstice and David Woodworth.

Thank you both for the help you have provided.

ISBN 0-9551256-0-X: 978-0-9551256-0-7

Published by Musker, Denby and Hirtzel,
Mozart at 250, P.O. Box 626, Hook RG27 7BW

Designed and typeset by Oxford Designers & Illustrators   www.o-d-i.com

Printed in Great Britain by Biddles Ltd, King's Lynn

INTRODUCTION

Mozart at 250 is a most valuable publication. Roger Musker's book presents the reader with Köchel's catalogue, supported by Einstein's subsequent emendations, but in a new light. With its cogent and succinct preface and prefatory list of works arranged according to genre, the main body of the work is fascinating, as we are led from K1 to the valedictory Requiem K626 by means of reviews and commentaries by Mozart's contemporaries, as well as extracts from the letters of the Mozart family. By means of the latter, Roger Musker comes as near as anyone has to 'working with Mozart' on a daily basis; the chronological journey across Europe comes alive, and the importance of London for Mozart, particularly when his later plan to live there failed to come to fruition, is deeply touching.

Under the heading, Posthumous Information, the author provides us with a set of contemporary obituaries to Mozart, telling and typically generous and modest comments by Haydn and memoirs of Mozart by the aged Goethe.

This book is vital for anyone who wishes to understand the circumstances in which Mozart lived, worked, thought and observed life (this is, after all, the composer of *Figaro*), especially where a comparison with musical life since the late eighteenth century is concerned. It has the advantage over some recent biographical studies in letting the development of Mozart's mind and career unfold without added layers of interpretation, and I find this aspect of Roger Musker's work most refreshing.

Dr Robert Saxton
University Lecturer
Fellow and Tutor in Music
Worcester College
Oxford

PREFACE

This book outlines in numerical order all Amadeus Mozart's (A.M.'s) works (not fragments/spurious) from K1 to K626, as outlined by the original *Köchel Catalogue* and Alfred Einstein's alterations in 1946.

In 1850 the amateur musicologist Ludwig Friedrich von Köchel, a botanist, started to categorise all A.M.'s works, arranging them in strictly chronological order from the very earliest work K1 in 1761 to the requiem K626. He used various sources and A.M.'s own thematic catalogue. In each work the first five bars were notated, publishing the *Köchel Catalogue* in 1862. This system is still the basis of the K numbers, although there have been six further revisions, particularly Alfred Einstein's published in 1946, which is used in this book.

This is a quick numerical reference guide showing the title, the scoring, when the work was completed (from A.M.'s own thematic catalogue which he started in 1782 and many other sources), where and for whom it was composed if known, the first performances, letter extracts and further relevant information specific to each K number. The extracts from the Mozart family letters as originally compiled by Maria Anna Basle, A.M's cousin, are taken with permission from Emily Anderson's *The Letters of Mozart and His Family* (London, Macmillan 1938, 3/1985), and further extracts from Otto Deutsch's documentary biography *Mozart* (Simon & Schuster 1964, 3/1990).

In the text:

A.M. is Amadeus Mozart.

L.M. is Leopold Mozart *(father)*.

N.M. is Nannerl Mozart *(sister)*.

C.M. is Constance Mozart *(wife)*.

The figure in brackets after each K number is the average playing time (Zaslaw/Fein). The principal currencies in circulation in Austria in A.M.'s lifetime were the gulden (or florin) and the ducat. There were four gulden in one ducat. In 1791 £500 was the equivalent to 4,883 gulden, or between 8 and 9 gulden to one English pound sterling. Therefore, for example, the fee for composing *The Marriage of Figaro* (K492), 450 gulden, was approximately £46 sterling.

Categories of music by
numerical Köchel numbers

PIANO VARIATIONS

1 - 2 - 3 - 4 - 5 - 24 - 25 - 54 - 94 - 153 - 154 - 179 - 180 - 264 - 265 - 352 -
353 - 354 - 355 - 394 - 395 - 396 - 397 - 398 - 399 - 400 - 401 - 455 - 460 -
475 - 485 - 494 - 500 - 511 - 533 - 540 - 573 - 574 - 613 - 624

(40)

PIANO AND STRINGS

6 - 7 - 8 - 9 - 10 - 11 - 12 - 13 - 14 - 15 - 26 - 27 - 28 - 29 - 30 - 31 - 55 - 56 -
57 - 58 - 59 - 60 - 61 - 107 - 296 - 301 - 302 - 303 - 304 - 305 - 306 - 359 - 360 -
372 - 376 - 377 - 378 - 379 - 380 - 402 - 403 - 404 - 442 - 454 - 478 - 481 -
493 - 496 - 502 - 526 - 542 - 547 - 548 - 564

(54)

SYMPHONIES

16 - 17 - 18 - 19 - 22 - 43 - 45 - 48 - 73 - 74 - 75 - 76 - 81 - 84 - 95 - 96 - 97 -
98 - 102 - 110 - 112 - 114 - 120 - 121 - 124 - 128 - 129 - 130 - 132 - 133 -
134 - 161 - 162 - 163 - 181 - 182 - 183 - 184 - 199 - 200 - 201 - 202 - 297 -
318 - 319 - 338 - 385 - 409 - 425 - 444 - 504 - 543 - 550 - 551.

(54)

SACRED WORKS

20 - 35 - 42 - 44 - 47 - 67 - 68 - 69 - 72 - (85) - 89 - 90 - 91 - 92 - 93 - 108 -
109 - 117 - 118 - 125 - 127 - 141 - 144 - 145 - 165 - 177 - 193 - 195 - 197 - 198 -
212 - 221 - 222 - 223 - 224 - 225 - 241 - 243 - 244 - 245 - 260 - 263 - 273 - 274 -
275 - 276 - 277 - 278 - 321 - 322 - 323 - 324 - 325 - 326 - 327 - 328 - 329 - 336 -
339 - 340 - 341 - 342 - 343 - 347 - 348 - 469

(66)

SONGS

21 - 23 - 52 - 53 - 142 - 147 - 148 - 149 - 150 - 151 - 152 - 226 - 227 - 228 -
229 - 230 - 231 - 232 - 233 - 234 - 235 - 236 - 349 - 350 - 351 - 383 - 390 -
391 - 392 - 393 - 443 - 472 - 473 - 474 - 476 - 507 - 508 - 517 - 518 - 519 - 520 -
523 - 524 - 529 - 530 - 531 - 552 - 553 - 554 - 555 - 556 - 557 - 558 - 559 - 560 -
561 - 562 - 569 - 596 - 597 - 598

(61)

MASSES
33 - 34 - 49 - 65 - 66 - 115 - 116 - 139 - 140 - 167 - 192 - 194 - 220 - 257 - 258 -
259 - 262 - 317 - 337 - 427

(20)

↓
Coronation Mass

VOICE AND ORCHESTRA
36 - 62 - 70 - 71 - 77 - 78 - 79 - 82 - 83 - 86 - 88 - 119 - 143 - 146 - 178 - 209 -
210 - 217 - 255 - 256 - 272 - 294 - 295 - 307 - 308 - 316 - 346 - 368 - 369 - 374 -
389 - 416 - 418 - 419 - 420 - 429 - 431 - 432 - 433 - 434 - 435 - 436 - 437 - 438 -
439 - 440 - 441 - 479 - 480 - 489 - 490 - 505 - 512 - 513 - 528 - 532 - 538 - 539 -
541 - 577 - 578 - 579 - 580 - 582 - 583 - 584 - 612 - 615 - 618 - 619 - 625

(71)

for
3 pianos
No 10   *No 11 No 12*

PIANO CONCERTOS
37 - 39 - 40 - 41 - 175 - 238 - 242 - 246 - 271 - 365 - 382 - 386 - 413 - 414 -
415 - 449 - 450 - 451 - 453 - 456 - 459 - 466 - 467 - 482 - 488 - 491 - 503 -
537 - 595   *15   16   17   20   19   22   23   24   25*
16   29   *18   20*
                                          all
OPERA   *29*
38 - 50 - 51 - 87 - 111 - 126 - 135 - 196 - 208 - 344 - 345 - 366 - 384 - 422 -
430 - 486 - 492 - 527 - 588 - 620 - 621

(29)

(21)

STRINGS – DUO, TRIO, QUARTET, QUINTET.
46 - 80 - 136 - 137 - 138 - 155 - 156 - 157 - 158 - 159 - 160 - 168 - 169 - 170 -
171 - 172 - 173 - 174 - 266 - 364 - 387 - 405 - 406 - 421 - 423 - 424 - 428 - 458 -
464 - 465 - 499 - 515 - 516 - 525 - 546 - 549 - 575 - 589 - 590 - 593 - 614

(41)

↓
the Dissonance

SERENADE - DIVERTIMENTO - CASSATION - MINUET - NOCTURNO
63 - 64 - 99 - 100 - 101 - 103 - 104 - 105 - 113 - 122 - 131 - 164 - 166 - 176 -
185 - 186 - 187 -188 - 190 - 191 - 203 - 204 - 205 - 213 - 239 - 240 - 247 - 250 -
251 - 252 - 253 - 254 - 270 - 286 - 287 - 288 - 289 - 320 - 334 - 361 - 388 - 443 -
452 - 461 - 522 - 563 - 568 - 585 - 599 - 601 - 604

(51)

DANCE

106 - 123 - 267 - 363 - 462 - 463 - 509 - 510 - 534 - 535 - 536 - 565 - 567 - 571 -
586 - 587 - 600 - 602 - 603 - 605 - 606 - 607 - 609 - 610 - 611

(25)

MARCH

189 - 206 - 214 - 215 - 237 - 248 - 249 - 290 - 335 - 362 - 408 - 445 - 544

(13)

VIOLIN CONCERTO

207 - 211 - 216 - 218 - 219 - 261 - 268 - 269 - 373 - 470

(10)

PIANO SONATA

279 - 280 - 281 - 282 - 283 - 284 - 292 - 309 - 310 - 311 - 312 - 330 - 331 -
332 - 333 - 457 - 545 - 570 - 576

(19)

WIND AND STRINGS

285 - 292 - 293 - 298 - 299 - 313 - 314 - 315 - 370 - 371 - 375 - 407 - 410 - 412 -
417 - 447 - 487 - 495 - 498 - 514 - 581 - 622

(22)

BALLET

300 - 367 - 446

(3)

GLASS HARMONICA

356 - 617

(2)

PIANO SONATA FOR FOUR HANDS

357 - 358 - 381 - 426 - 448 - 497 - 501 - 521

(8)

MASONIC MUSIC
411 - 468 - 471 - 477 - 483 - 484 - 506 - 623

                                                                    (8)

ARRANGEMENTS
566 - 572 - 591 - 592 (85)

                                                                    (4)

MECHANICAL ORGAN
594 - 608 - 616

                                                                    (3)

REQUIEM
626

                                                                    (1)
                                                                  ─────
                                                                    626

MOZART

250th Anniversary 1756-(1791)-2006

Numerical Köchel numbers K1–K626

K1 SOLO PIANO.   A.M. early composition, written in Salzburg in 1761/2 in L.M.'s handwriting. K1 is a series of six short dance-like works of a simple construction (A.M. aged 5 in 1761).

L.M. wrote:

"… compositions by Wolfganerl in the first three months after his fifth birthday."

i.e. between February and April 1761. Born 27 January 1756 (6)

K2 MINUET FOR PIANO IN F MAJOR.   Written in Salzburg in January 1762 (1).

K3 ALLEGRO FOR PIANO IN B FLAT.   Written in Salzburg 4 March 1762 (1).

K4 MINUET FOR PIANO IN F MAJOR.   Written in Salzburg 5 July 1762 (1).

K5 MINUET FOR PIANO IN C MAJOR.   Written in Salzburg 5 July 1762 (1).

K6 SONATA FOR PIANO AND VIOLIN IN D MAJOR.   Written in Salzburg in 1762/3 (14).

K7 SONATA FOR PIANO AND VIOLIN IN D MAJOR.   Written in Paris in 1764 under the influence of John Eckardt, a Parisian harpsichord player. Both K6 and K7 dedicated to Victoire, second daughter of Louis XV (14).

Extract letter 23, L.M. to Hagenauer (landlord in Salzburg), Paris, 22 February 1764:

"In a fortnight at latest we shall drive out again to Versailles, in order that we may present to Madam Victoire, the King's second daughter, to whom it

[K6, K7] *has been dedicated (the first work of the engraved sonatas of the great M. Wolfgang) … We have tilled the soil well and now hope for a good harvest. But one must take things as they come. I should have had at least twelve Louis D'Or if my children had not had to stay at home for a few days. Thank God they are better."*

K8   SONATA FOR PIANO AND VIOLIN IN B FLAT.   Written in Salzburg 1763 (13).

K9   SONATA FOR PIANO AND VIOLIN IN G MAJOR.   Written in Paris in 1764. K8 and K9 dedicated to Countess de Tesse.

Extract letter 33, L.M. to Hagenauer, London, 3 December 1764:
"I regret that a few mistakes have remained in the engraving, even after the first corrections were made … in the last trio you will find three consecutive fifths in the violin part, which my young gentleman perpetuated and which, although I corrected them, old Vendome left in. On the other hand, they are proof that our little Wolfgang composed them himself which perhaps quite naturally, everybody will not believe."

These piano and violin sonatas were played by A.M. and his sister Nannerl (aged 11) in The Little Theatre, Haymarket, London on 21 February 1765. They were also played in Hickford's Great Room in Brewer Street on Monday 13 May. Tickets five shillings each, bought from Mr Mozart (L.M.) at Mr Williamson's in Thrift Street, Soho.

The first recorded public performance was 1 October 1762 at The Trinity in Linz, on a trip with the family down The Danube.

Some comments of A.M's playing skills
Count Zinzendorf's diary 9 October 1762 is the first written acknowledgement of A.M. as a public performer:
"… in the evening, at 8 o'clock I called for Lamberg and we went to Colaltto's together where La Bianchi sang, and a little boy, who, it is said, is but five and a half years of age, played the harpsichord."

Then again from Zinzendorf's diary 17 October 1762:
"… then at Thun's, where the little child from Salzburg and his sister, played the harpsichord. The poor little fellow played marvellously, he is a child of spirit, lively, charming, his sisters' playing also masterly, and he applauded her. Mlle de Gudenus who plays the harpsichord well, gave him a kiss, and he wiped his face …"

A.M. early biographer, Niermetschek:

"... his admirable dexterity, which particularly in the left hand and the bass were considered quite unique, his feeling and delicacy and beautiful expression were the attractions of his playing ... and this made A.M. the greatest pianist of his time."

Clementi in 1782 wrote:

"... until then I had never heard anyone perform with such spirit and grace. I was particularly astonished by an adagio and some of his extemporised variations."

Extract letter 241, A.M. to L.M., 13 November 1777:

"I entered during a kyrie and played the end of it. After the priest had intoned the Gloria I played a cadenza. Because this was all so different from what they were accustomed to hear, they all turned round ... now and then was a pizzicato. And each time I just brushed the keys. I was in the best of spirits ... I took the subject of the Sanctus and treated it as a fugue. Everyone stood there and stared at me. The pedal is different from ours, that put me off at first, but I soon understood how it worked."

Albrechtsbergour wrote:

"His improvisations were well ordered as if he had them lying written out before him. This led several to think that when he performed an improvisation in public, he must have thought everything out and practised it beforehand. One evening they [A.M.] met at a musical soiree, A.M. was in a good mood and demanded a theme from A. The latter provided him with an old German popular song. A.M. sat down and improvised on this theme for an hour in such a way as to excite general admiration, and show that by means of variations and fugues in which he never departed from the theme that he was a master of every aspect of the musicians art."

From a Prague 1808 newspaper report:

"It was his piano playing that first won admirers and devotees; for although Vienna had a great many masters on the instrument, the public's favourite, none of them could compare with our Mozart. A remarkable quickness, which particularly in consideration of his left hand or bass could be called unique, neatness and delicacy the most beautiful, most eloquent expression, and a sensitivity that went straight to the heart ... these were the qualities of his playing which with the richness of his invention and his profound knowledge of composition, technique, could not help captivating every hearer and raising Mozart to the greatest key-board player of his age

... indeed we do not know what to admire the more – the extraordinary composition or the extraordinary playing. No one can imagine this pleasure to hear Mozart play the most difficult scores with his own inimitable skill and even sing the while and correct the mistakes of others could not but excite the greatest admiration."

Critic Richard Kelly, London 1826:

"... and what was to me one of the greatest gratifications of my musical life, was there introduced to that prodigy of nature, Mozart. He favoured the company of performers. His feeling, the rapidity of his fingers, and the great execution and strength of his left hand particularly, and the apparent inspiration of his modulations astounded me ... He was so particular when he played, that if the slightest noise were made, he instantly left off."

Kelly further continues in 1830:

"I was witnessed of so many of the arts of his masterly hand when he sat at the piano. Rich in invention and dazzling as his fantasies were they yet never lacked the greatest clarity in their perfect contrapuntal purity."

Goethe wrote in 1830:

"... we spoke about Mozart. I saw him when he was a 7 year old boy, when he gave a concert on my way through. I was myself was about 14 years old and I can still quite clearly remember that little fellow with his wig and sword."

In 1852 Goethe, remembering A.M., wrote:

"I played him a fantasia of his own composition. Not bad he said to my astonishment. Now I'll play it for you. What a wonder! The piano became a completely different instrument under his fingers; he had it amplified by means of a second key."

K10   SONATA FOR PIANO, VIOLIN AND CELLO IN B FLAT.

K11   SONATA FOR PIANO, VIOLIN AND CELLO IN G MAJOR.

K12   SONATA FOR PIANO, VIOLIN AND CELLO IN A MAJOR.

K13   SONATA FOR PIANO, VIOLIN AND CELLO IN F MAJOR.

K14   SONATA FOR PIANO, VIOLIN AND CELLO IN C MAJOR.

K15   SONATA FOR PIANO, VIOLIN AND CELLO IN B FLAT.   Written in London in 1764 and dedicated to Queen Charlotte, wife of George III. On 18 January 1765 A.M. received fifty guineas from the Queen (64).

Extract letter 32, L.M. to Hagenauer, London, 27 November 1764:
> *"… in addition I have the heavy expense of having six sonatas [K10–K15] of our master Wolfgang engraved and printed which at her own request are being dedicated to the Queen of Great Britain."*

K16   SYMPHONY NO 1 IN E FLAT in three movements.   Scored for 2 oboe: 2 horn: strings. Written in London in August/September 1764, and first performed on 21 February 1765 in The Little Theatre, Haymarket (see also page 9) (13).

[handwritten margin note: age 8. Hard to believe]

Extract letter 30, L.M. to Hagenauer, London, 9 August 1764:
> *"I and the family are now in a spot outside the town* [182 Ebury Street or 180 Ebury Street, Chelsea]. *It has one of the most beautiful views in the world. Where ever I turn my eyes I only see gardens and in the distance the finest castles, and the house in which I am living has a lovely garden."*

Extract letter 39, L.M. to Hagenauer, London, 8 February 1765
> *"Oh, what a lot of things I have to do. The symphonies at the concert* [K16 & K19] *will all be played by Wolfgang. I must copy them out myself, unless I want to pay a shilling for each sheet. Copying music is a very profitable business here."*

K17   SYMPHONY NO 2 IN B FLAT.

K18   SYMPHONY NO 3 IN E FLAT.   Possibly by or in conjunction with Abel. There is doubt about this work.

K19   SYMPHONY NO 4 IN D MAJOR.   Scored for 2 oboe: 2 horn: strings. Written in London in 1765 and performed with K16 on 21 February 1765 in The Little Theatre, Haymarket, London (9).

K20   MADRIGAL IN G MAJOR, *God Is Our Refuge*.   Scored for S: A: T: B (Soprano: Alto: Tenor: Bass): choir. Written in London in July 1765, partly in L.M.'s handwriting. The manuscript of this work was presented to the British Museum as an example of A.M.'s early work. In English, the only time he wrote in this language, in which both he and his sister had been taking lessons.

Extract letter from the secretary of the British Museum, Mr M. Matey, 19 July 1765

"I am ordered by the standing of The British Museum, to signify to you [L.M.] that they had received the present of the musical performances of your very ingenious son which you were pleased lately to make, and return your thanks for the same."

This manuscript presentation to the BM was as a result of a visit to the family by the Reverend Andrew Planta, the assistant keeper of printed books at the BM, on 19 July 1765. This manuscript is now available for public viewing in the public library of the British Museum.

K21   ARIA FOR TENOR, *Va, dal furor portata.*   Scored for 2 oboe: 2 bassoon: 2 horn: strings. Written in London in 1765, text by Metastasio (6).

There are two surviving copies of this aria, one of them with L.M.'s corrections and suggestions.

In a letter in 1768 L.M. says:

"I asked someone to take any portion of the works of Metastasio, open the book and put before little Wolfgang the first aria he should hit upon. Wolfgang took a pen and with the most amazing rapidity, without hesitation ..."

The Mozart Family in London

On 23 April 1764 the Mozart family arrived in London. A.M. was accompanied by his parents (his mother and L.M. his father) and Nannerl (N.M.), his sister; she was eleven years old, he eight.

They stayed their first night in London at the White Bear Coaching Inn, Piccadilly. Moving into lodgings on 24 April with a barber/surgeon, John Couzin, at 19 Cecil Court, St Martin's Lane. On 27 April A.M. and N.M. were received and performed for George III and Queen Charlotte; L.M. received 24 guineas.

Extract letter 27, L.M. to Hagenauer, London, 28 May 1764, about 27 April:

"... we were with the King and Queen in the Queen's palace [now Buckingham Palace] *in St James's Park; so that by the fifth day after our arrival we were already at court. The present was only 24 guineas ... but the graciousness with which both His Majesty and Her Majesty received us cannot be described."*

Extract letter to the Earl of Huntingdon from Claude Helvetius, Paris, 1764:
"Allow me to ask your protection for one of the most singular beings in
existence. He is a little German prodigy who has arrived in London
these last few days. He plays and composes on the spot the most difficult
and the most agreeable pieces for harpsichord. He is the most eloquent
and the most profound composer of his kind. His father's name is Mozart
... he lodges with this prodigy, aged 7, with Mr Couzin, hare cutter in
Cecil Court. All Paris and the whole of France were enchanted with this
little boy."

On 17 May A.M. gave a concert at Hichford's Great Room, Brewer Street.
Tickets were a guinea each.

Extract *Public Advertiser*, London, 9 May 1764:
"Concerto on the harpsichord by Master Mozart, who is a real prodigy of
Nature; he is but seven years of age [L.M. made him a year younger, he
was eight] plays anything at sight and composes amazingly well."

A.M. and N.M. performed again at court on 19 May, A.M. playing the organ,
and again the fee was 24 guineas.

After a short illness the children played again in public on 5 June 1764.

Extract *Public Advertiser*, London, 31 May 1764:
"At the Great Room in Spring Room near St James's Park Tuesday 5 June
will be performed a grand concert of vocal and instrumental music.
For the benefit of Miss Mozart and Master Mozart, seven years of age,
prodigies of Nature; taking the opportunity of representing to the public
the greatest prodigy that Europe or that Human Nature has to boast of.
Everybody will be astonished to hear a child of such tender Age playing the
harpsichord in such perfection ... it is hard to express which is more
astonishing, his execution upon the harpsichord, playing at sight, or his
own composition."

Extract *Public Advertiser*, London, 1 June 1764:
"Everybody will be struck with Admiration to hear them, and particularly
to hear a young Boy of seven years of age play on the harpsichord with
such dexterity and perfection. It surpasses all understanding or all
imagination."

The tickets were a guinea each, the expenses 20 guineas, box office receipts
100 guineas.

Extract letter 28, L.M. to Hagenauer, London, 8 June 1764:

"I have had another shock, that is the shock of taking 100 guineas in three hours ... June 5th was the only day on which a concert could be attempted, because the king's birthday was on the 4th and the reason why we gave it then was in order to become known."

A charity concert was held on Friday 29 June at Ranelagh House to raise money for a womens' hospital.

Extract letter 29, L.M. to Hagenauer, London, 28 June 1764:

"On Friday 29th June, that is on the feast of St Peter and St Paul, there will be a concert or benefit at Ranelaugh in aid of a newly established hospital de femmes en couche and whoever wishes to attend must pay 5 shillings entrance. I am letting Wolfgang play a concerto on the organ at this concert ... that is, you see, one way of winning the affection of this quite exceptional nation."

Extract *Public Advertiser*, London, 26 June 1764:

"In the course of the evening's entertainments, the celebrated and astonishing Master Mozart, lately arrived a child of seven years of age, will perform several fine select Pieces of his own Composition on the Harpsichord and on the organ, which has already given the highest pleasure, delight and surprise to the greatest judges of music in England or Italy and is justly esteemed the most extraordinary prodigy, and most amazing Genius that has appeared in any age ..."

L.M. fell dangerously ill on 8 July 1764.

Extract letter 30, L.M. to Hagenauer, London, 3 August 1764:

"Do not be frightened! But prepare your heart to hear one of the saddest events. Perhaps you will have already noticed my condition from my handwriting. Almighty God has visited me ... with a sudden and severe illness ... and which I feel too weak to describe."

To aid his recovery the family moved out of central London on 6 August and lodged with the Randel family at 5 Fields Row, Chelsea, which is now 180 (or 182) Ebury Street (180 and 182 were possibly one house in 1764; it is now called Mozart Terrace) (see K16).

Memoirs of N.M., 22 January 1800, Leipzig, when recalling their time in London:

"In London, where our father lay dangerously ill, we were forbidden to touch the piano. And so, in order to occupy himself, my brother composed his first symphony [K16] for all the instruments of the orchestra; but especially for trumpet and kettle drums. I had to copy out as I sat at his side. Whilst he composed and I copied he said to me 'remind me to give the horn something worthwhile to do!' He loved his parents, especially his father, so dearly, that he composed a melody which he would sing out loud each day; his father had to sit him on a chair. Father always had to sing the second part ... when the ceremony was over, he would kiss his father most tenderly and go to bed very peacefully and contentedly."

They remained at Ebury Street until 25 September 1764 when the family took lodgings at Thomas Williamson's house at 15 Thrift Street (now Frith Street, Soho). Williamson was a corset maker.

Extract letter 31, L.M. to Hagenauer, Chelsea near London, 13 September 1764:

"I now state that every day, although my progress is slow, I am feeling a little better ... so that you may know how my illness started, I must tell you that in England there is a kind of native complaint which is called a cold. That is why you hardly ever see people wearing summer clothes. They all wear cloth garments yet until 14th July although I did not feel very well, I went about and tried to cure myself by perspiring, which is the remedy generally adopted here ... once I leave England, I shall never see guineas again, so we must make the most of our opportunity."

On 25 October 1764 the whole family were received a third time at court resulting in the dedication of K10 to K15 to Queen Charlotte on 18 January 1765:

"Title and dedication in London; six sonatas for the harpsichord which can be played with the accompaniment of Violin or transverse Flute, very humbly dedicated to Her Majesty Charlotte, Queen of Great Britain. Composed by I.G. Wolfgang Mozart, aged 8 years. Opus III London printed for the author and sold at his lodgings at Mr Williamson in Thrift Street Soho."

A copy is deposited in the British Library.

Extract letter 34, L.M. to Hagenauer, London, 8 February 1765:

"On the evening of the 15th we are giving a concert which will probably bring in about 150 guineas. Whether I shall still make anything after that, and if so what, I do not know."

Extract *Public Advertiser*, London, 14 February 1765:

> "On account of Dr Arne's oratorio of Judith performers Master Mozart and
> Miss Mozart are obliged to postpone the Concert which should have been
> tomorrow, the 15th instant to the 18th instant. They desire that the Nobility
> and Gentry will be so kind to excuse them for not performing according to
> the time first proposed."

The concert was again postponed from 18 to 21 February at The Little
Theatre, Haymarket.

Extract letter 35, L.M. to Hagenauer, London, 19 March 1765:

> *"My concert, which I intended to give on 15 th February, did not take place*
> *until 21 st on account of the number of entertainments which really weary*
> *one here, was not well attended as I had hoped. Nevertheless I took in about*
> *130 guineas. As however the expenses connected with it amounted to over 27*
> *guineas I have not made much more that 100 guineas ... I will not bring up*
> *my children in such a dangerous place where the majority of inhabitants*
> *have no religion and where one only has an evil example before one. You*
> *would be amazed if you saw how children are brought up here, not to*
> *mention other matters concerned with religion."*

L.M. and A.M. had been offered a proposal to stay in London which he turned
down.

Extract *Public Advertiser*, London, 11 March 1765:

> "By desire. For the benefit of Master Mozart of eight years and Miss Mozart
> of twelve years of age, prodigies of Nature, before their departure form
> England, which will be in six weeks time, there will be performed at the
> end of this month or the beginning of April a Concert of Vocal and
> Instrumental music. Tickets at half a guinea each ... to be had of Mister
> Mozart and Mister Williamson's at Thrift Street, Soho. Where those Ladies
> and Gentleman who will honour him with their company from 12 to 3 in
> the afternoon any day of the week, except Tuesday and Friday, may by
> taking each a ticket gratify their curiosity, and not only hear this young
> Music Master and his Sister perform in private, but likewise try his
> surprising musical capacity by giving him any Thing to play by sight, or
> any music without Base which he will write upon the Spot without
> recurring to his harpsichord."

The family hoped to leave London early in June, but this had to be
postponed.

Extract letter 36, L.M. to Hagenauer, London, 18 April 1765:

> *"As for my departure with the family, I have no more definite news; and any sensible person must realise that it is not an easy matter to decide. It will take us all our time to get away from here … We have been in England for a whole year. Why, we have practically made our home here. So that to take our departure from England requires even more preparation that when we left Salzburg."*

In June 1765 the Mozarts met Doctor Daines Barrington (a well known musicologist and critic), and later in November 1769 in writing a letter to Matthew Matey (see K20) he wrote:

> "… the instance which I now desire you will communicate to the Royal Society, that learned body as of an early execution of an extraordinary musical talent; born 27th January 1756 at 8pm in Salzburg he came over to England , where he continued for more than a year. During this time I was witness of his most extraordinary abilities as a musician, both at some public concerts, and likewise having been alone with him for a considerable time in his father's house … I carried to him a manuscript duet … my intention was to have irrefutable proof of his abilities as a player at sight, it being impossible for him that he could have seen the music beforehand. The score was no sooner put upon his desk, than he began to play in a most masterly manner, as well as in time and style corresponding to the intensions of the composer. He then took the upper part, leaving the under one to his Father. His voice was thin and infantile, but nothing could exceed the masterly way he sang. His father was once or twice out on which occasions the son looked back with some anger pointing out to his father his mistakes, and setting him right."

It seems that by the age of nine there was very little else that L.M. could teach his son.

They were still in London on 9 July 1765, and the last notice in the *Public Advertiser* on that day again stated that A.M. and N.M. would perform daily from 12 until 3 o'clock in The Great Room at the Swan and Harp Tavern, Cornhill, 2s 6d per person, where the children would play together with four hands upon the same harpsichord with a handkerchief covering the keyboard.

Extract letter 37, L.M. to Hagenauer, London, 9 July 1765:

> *"No doubt you will be thinking that we have long ago swum over the sea. But it has been impossible to get away … I beg when you receive this letter*

to arrange immediately for six masses to be said ... these are to prepare our way over the sea."

On 24 July 1765 the family left London for Canterbury, staying with Sir Horace Mann (a relation of Horace Walpole) at Bourn Place. A.M. gave a public concert during his stay here and their last night in England attended a horse race where L.M. won some money. At 10am on 1 August they left Dover arriving in Calais at 1.30pm and stayed at the Hotel d'Angleterre.

A.M., despite numerous schemes, never returned to England.

K22   SYMPHONY NO 5 IN B FLAT.   Scored for 2 oboe: 2 horn: strings. Written in The Hague in December 1765 and performed in Amsterdam on 29 January 1766, A.M. conducting. Entrance price two florins (7).

Extract from an advertisement for the concert, 29 January 1766:
"A grand concert at the hall of the riding-school in Amsterdam, at which his son aged eight years and eleven months and his daughter aged fourteen will perform ... all the overtures will be of the composition of this little composer, who, never having found his like, was the Admiration of the courts of Vienna, Versailles and London ... music lovers may submit pieces of music to him at will, which he will perform entirely from the open book. Two florins person."

A second concert was held in the hall of the riding-school on 26 February:
"... universal contentment and satisfaction given by the children. Lovers of music desire a second concert again two florins."

K23   ARIA FOR SOPRANO, *Conservati Fedele*.   Accompaniment strings: written in The Hague in October 1765 and revised in January 1766. Text by Metastasio (4).

K24   PIANO VARIATIONS IN G MAJOR.   Based on a Dutch song. Written in The Hague in January 1766. Eight variations (5).

K25   PIANO VARIATIONS IN D MAJOR.   Written in Amsterdam in February 1766 on the old Dutch National Anthem (4).

Extract letter 41, L.M. to Hagenauer, Paris, 16 May 1766:
"In the same parcel there are two sets of variations, one of which little Wolfgang had to compose on an air, written on the occasion on the majority

and installation of the Prince of Orange ... the other set he dashed off
hurriedly, which everybody all over Holland is singing, playing and
whistling. They are trifles!"

An announcement in *The Hague Courant,* 7 March 1766:
> "... a Dutch song on the installation of the Prince of Orange (18 years) ...
> furnished with 8 artful variations by the celebrated young composer J.G.W.
> Mozart aged nine ... and the well known ditty for the clavier by the
> aforesaid young Mozart."

The festivities for the coming of age of the Prince of Orange lasted from 2 to
12 March and the two sets of variations were performed by the children at the
Dutch Court on 11 March to great acclaim.

K26   SONATA FOR PIANO AND VIOLIN IN E FLAT (8).

K27   SONATA FOR PIANO AND VIOLIN IN G MAJOR (9).

K28   SONATA FOR PIANO AND VIOLIN IN C MAJOR (9).

K29   SONATA FOR PIANO AND VIOLIN IN D MAJOR (8).

K30   SONATA FOR PIANO AND VIOLIN IN F MAJOR (9).

K31   SONATA FOR PIANO AND VIOLIN IN B FLAT (8).   Written in The
Hague in February 1766; dedicated and performed to the Prince of Orange's
sister, the Princess of Nassau-Weilborg.

Extract letter 41, L.M. to Hagenauer, Paris, 16 May 1766:
> *"From Amsterdam we return to The Hague for the festival of the Prince*
> *of Orange on which occasion our little composer was asked to turn*
> *out six sonatas [K26–K31] for the clavier and violin accompaniment*
> *for the Princess."*

K32   GALIMATHIAS MUSICUM.   Scored for harpsichord: 2 oboe: 2 horn:
2 bassoon: strings. Written in The Hague in February/March 1766 for the
installation of the Prince of Orange in March 1766. Eighteen short sketches
(12). There are in fact seventeen sketches, one missing. The last sketch is a
repeat of K25 (the Dutch National Anthem).

K33   KYRIE IN F MAJOR.   Scored for S: A: T: B: strings. Written in Paris 12 June 1766 (2). This is the first of the two complete kyries surviving; the other much finer and more mature work for chorus and orchestra is K341.

K34   OFFERTORY IN C MAJOR, *Scande Coeli Limina.*   Scored for S: choir: 2 trumpet: timpani: 2 violin: bass: organ. Written in Kloster-See in Bavaria early in 1767 as A.M.'s first Liturgical work and first performed 21 March 1767 in the Seeon Monastery on the feast of St Benedict (5).

K35   ORATORIO, *Die Schuldigkeit des Ernsten Gebotes* (The First Commandment).   Scored for 3 S: 2 T: 2 oboe/flute: 2 bassoon: 2 horn: trombone: strings. Written in Salzburg early 1767 and first performed in Salzburg 12 March 1767, text by Weiser. Michael Haydn, the son of Joseph Haydn, collaborated with A.M. in acts 2 and 3.

Minutes of Salzburg University, 12 March 1767:
> "Holiday. After dinner. At half past six in the main university hall there was sung an oratorio set to music by D. Wolfgang Mozart, aged ten and greatly skilled in composition set to music for five persons, text by Weiser."

On 18 March:
> "... to little Mozartl, for the composition of the music to an oratorio, a gold medal of twelve duckets ... 60 fl. This is the weight of twelve duckets, paid from Archbishop Colloredo's privy purse."

K36   RECITATIVE AND ARIA FOR FOUR TENORS, *Or Che Il Dover.*   Scored for solo T: 2 oboe: 2 bassoon: 2 horn: 2 trumpet: timpani: strings. Written in Salzburg in December 1766 on the anniversary of Archbishop Siegmund Von Schrattenbach's Coronation (10).

This and K70, written a year later, were composed to be sung during an operatic interval in honour of a celebrity, in this case the Archbishop.

Extract from the Salzburg Court diaries:
> "His Serene Highness betook himself to the opera ... lastly there was a licenza consisting of a recitative and aria, the music of which was composed to everybody's admiration by young Wolfgang Mozard ... a remarkable boy ten years of age, complete master of the harpsichord, and has only just arrived back here from England."

K37   CONCERTO FOR KEYBOARD IN F MAJOR (1).   Scored for solo harpsichord or piano, and arrangement from the work of H.F. Raupach, arranged in Salzburg in April 1767 (17).

This the first "piano concerto". K37 and K39 to K41 are arrangements of sonata movements by C.P.E. Bach, Raupach and Honauer. These four concerti were written between April and July 1767 in Salzburg. Raupach was a well known composer of operas, just returned from St Petersburg. He had met A.M. in Paris in 1766 and had a great influence on the child. Later Raupach wrote:

"... at the age of eleven years Mozart was already composing concerti of great structure. What will come later will be very interesting."

K38   MUSICAL COMEDY, *Apollo And Hyacinthus*.   Scored for 2 S: 2 A: T: B: 2 oboe: 2 horn: strings. Libretto by Widl. A Latin language school comedy commissioned by Salzburg University, and first performed on 13 May 1767 (60).

Extract from Hubner's diary, 13 May 1767:

"The music for this comedy was composed by the celebrated and extraordinary boy of eleven years old, Wolfgang Mozart, son of the noble and vigorous Leopold."

It was usual for students to be given the opportunity of arranging performances at the end of the academic year, before the prize giving. A.M., aged eleven, was of course far too young to be at university.

From the university archives;

"Monarchs will vie for their procession, they will not remain long in Salzburg. The father is not only a gifted musician, but a man of sense and good nature, and I have never seen a man of his profession so united and so much talent to so much merit. He was understandably responsible for nurturing the musical genius in his hands, and to cope with such a prodigy."

There is no doubt that L.M. must have been not only vigorous but an immensely able teacher, but to quote from him in an undated letter "... one of the most loveable of creatures imaginable who puts wit and spirit into everything he does, with all grace and sweetness of his age. He even reassures one with his gaiety against the fear that so premature a fruit might fall before it has come to maturity".

K39 PIANO CONCERTO NO 2 IN B FLAT.   Scored for piano: 2 oboe: 2 horn: strings. Written as an arrangement from H.F. Raupach in June 1767 (15).

K40 PIANO CONCERTO NO 3 IN D MAJOR.   Scored for solo keyboard (harpsichord/piano): 2 oboe: 2 horn: strings. As an arrangement from Hanauer Ekhardt and C.P.E. Bach, arrangements made in July 1767 in Salzburg (13).

K41 PIANO CONCERTO NO 4 IN G MAJOR.   Scored for solo keyboard: 2 oboe: 2 horn: strings. As an arrangement from Ekhardt and Raupach. Arrangement made in July 1767 in Salzburg (15).

K42 CANTATA, *Grab Musik.*   Scored for S: B: choir: 2 oboe: 2 horn: strings. Written in early 1767 and first performed in Salzburg Cathedral on 7 April 1767; with further editions in 1773. This work was a test piece for A.M. from Salzburg University to show his ability in unaided composition (23).

K43 SYMPHONY NO 6 IN F MAJOR.   Scored for 2 oboe/flute: 2 horn: strings. Written in December 1767 in Vienna, with the first performance on 30 December 1767 at Brunn (this is not certain but most likely) (17).

K44 ANTIPHON CIBAVIT EOS IN A MAJOR.   Scored for S: A: T: B: organ. Written in 1770.

K45 SYMPHONY NO 7 IN D MAJOR in four movements.   Scored for 2 oboe: 2 trumpet: timpani: strings. Written in Vienna 16 June 1768 and used as the overture to *La Finta Semplice* (K51) (12).

K46 STRING QUINTETS IN C AND F MAJOR.   Written in Vienna, 1 September 1768 (11).

K47 OFFERTORY IN C MAJOR, *Vene Sancte Spiritus.*   Scored for solo S: A: T: B: chorus; 2 oboe: 2 horn: 2 trumpet: timpani. Written in Vienna in the autumn of 1768 (6).

This offertory was performed, on 10 December 1768, at a consecration of the newly built church of the orphanage on the Renweg, Vienna:

> "The whole of the music for this solemnity by Wolfgang Mozart, the little son, aged twelve, but already well known for his talents."

K48   SYMPHONY NO 8 IN D MAJOR.   Scored for 2 oboe: 2 horn: 2 trumpet: timpani: strings. Written in Vienna 13 December 1768 (16).

These three symphonies K43, K45 and K48 are grouped together, showing local influences, and were the end of "boyhood" symphonies as the next (K73) was four years later.

K49   MASS IN G MAJOR.   Scored for solo S: A: T: B: choir: 3 trombones: strings: organ. Written in Vienna in the autumn of 1768 (18).

Extract letter 70, A.M. to his pupil Katherl Gilowsky (she was also a relation to Hagenauer and his first student). Written in Latin in Salzburg in 1769, precise date not known:

"I should like to know for what reason idleness is so popular with most young people that it is impossible to draw them from it either by words or punishment."

During this time A.M. was learning Latin, French, English and Italian. German was his mother tongue.

K50   BASTIEN AND BASTIENNE.   Singspiel opera, spoken dialogue broken by music. Scored for solo S: T: B: 2 oboe/flute: 2 horn: strings. Commissioned by Dr Mesmer, the famous hypnotist, in the summer of 1768 and first performed in his garden theatre in October 1768. Mesmerism was also used in *Cosi Fan Tutti* (see K588) (45).

The first performance in September or October 1768 was not complete, and the second, which took place on 23 April 1777 at Augsburg, was the last performance for 122 years, the next taking place in Berlin in 1890.

Dr Anton Mesmer had married a very rich wife. He built a theatre in the grounds of his house and supported A.M. considerably at this time.

K51   LA FINTA SEMPLICE (The Simple Pretence).   Comic opera scored for 3 S: 2 T: 2 B : 2 flute/horn: 2 oboe: strings. Libretto by Solteccini. Written in mid 1768 and first performed on 1 May 1769 in the Archbishop of Salzburg's palace (166).

Extract letter 55, L.M. to Hagenauer, Vienna, 3 February 1768:

"And where is my boy more likely to succeed than in the theatre? But of course the opera [K51] *will not be performed until after Easter. So it is an operabuffa* [buffa means comic] *but not a short one for this is to last about*

> *two and a half or three hours. There are no singers here for serious opera even for Gluck's serious opera ..."*

The first performance in May 1769, having been delayed by the Impresario Afflisco who, having paid A.M. 100 ducats, seemed to get cold feet over the first performance and wanted to abandon the project entirely. L.M. persuaded him to continue with the first performance.

K52 SONG, *Daphne Diene Rosenwangen.*

K53 SONG, *Freude Konigen Der Weisen* (Joy Queen of the wise) in F major. Written in Vienna in the autumn of 1768, words by J.P. Uz. Composed for the young daughter of Dr Wolf, the physician to the Archbishop.

Both this song and K52 were published in Vienna in December 1768 in a children's "comic". Both piano accompaniment. During this period there was a large market for simple compositions able to be played at home. These two songs became very popular but due to non-existent copyright, A.M. received no financial benefit.

K54 VARIATIONS FOR PIANO IN F MAJOR (9).

K55 SONATA FOR PIANO AND VIOLIN IN F MAJOR (spurious – *not genuine*).

K56 SONATA FOR PIANO AND VIOLIN IN C MAJOR (dubious – *doubtful*).

K57 SONATA FOR PIANO AND VIOLIN IN F MAJOR (dubious).

K58 SONATA FOR PIANO AND VIOLIN IN E FLAT (dubious).

K59 SONATA FOR PIANO AND VIOLIN IN C MINOR (dubious).

K60 SONATA FOR PIANO AND VIOLIN IN E MINOR (dubious).

K61 SONATA FOR PIANO AND VIOLIN; arrangement of a sonata by Raupach.

K62 CASSATION IN D MAJOR.   Scored for 2 oboe: 2 horn: 2 trumpet: strings. Written in Salzburg in 1769 and used in K87 – *Mitridate* (4).

Extract letter 106, A.M. to N.M., Bologna, 4 August 1770:
> *"There, I have granted your request. I hardly think it can be one of*
> *my compositions, for who would dare to pass off as his own a*
> *composition by the Kapellmeister's son, whose mother and sister are*
> *in Salzburg."*

K63   SERENADE IN G MAJOR in seven movements.   Scored for 2 oboe: 2 horn: strings. Written in Salzburg in 1769, influenced by Haydn's G Major Symphony No. 23, and first performed on 8 August 1769 at Physicians Music Gymnasium in Salzburg. Also performed the Serenade in C Major, which is now lost (24).

Extract from Hagenauer's calendar, 8 August 1769.
> "... today there was a physicians final-musik, composed by Wolfganus
> Mozart. The final music was always given on a Wednesday at the end of
> the academic year by students of the philosophical faculty."

K64   MINUET FOR ORCHESTRA IN D MAJOR.

K65   MASS IN D MINOR.   Scored for solo S: A: T: B: choir: strings: organ. Written in Salzburg 14 January 1769 and first performed at the Collegiate Church, Salzburg on 5 February 1769 (15).

Extract letter 69, L.M. to Archbishop Von Schrattenbach of Salzburg, 8 March 1769:
> *"... as my stay in Vienna has nevertheless taken place against my will and to*
> *my disadvantage and as I could not leave Vienna before without loss of my*
> *honour and that of my child, and as, in addition, both my son and I have*
> *composed various works* [K49, K65, K139] *for the church and especially for*
> *use in your cathedral."*

Extract from Hagenauer's calendar, 5 February 1769:
> "... at 9 o'clock in the Collegiate Church his Reverence celebrated mass in
> the presence of the Prince (Archbishop); the music of the mass was
> composed by Dom. Wolfganus Mozart, a youth of thirteen."

A poem written at this time by a passer-by and published in a Salzburg newspaper in February 1769:
> *A child, by nature formed a work of art,*
> *A wondrous boy, one fortunate day was born,*

Whose genius turned the Father of the past
They praised the happy land that gave the birth
And look with envy on their native town.
Now let me wish, indeed if wish I may
That thou may'st live for ever in men's hearts
Thou could'st thyself be immortal like thy art
If maturity assured let the native town of Salzburg
Let him down.

A.M. always felt he was undervalued in Salzburg and ultimately "kicked down the stairs" by Hieronymus Colloredo, who later became Archbishop of Salzburg.

K66   MASS IN C MAJOR, *Dominicus.*   Scored for solo S: A: T: B: choir: 2 oboe: 2 horn: trumpet: timpani: strings. Written in Salzburg in October 1769 for Cajetan Dominicus Hagenauer, who had just entered the monastery of St Peter Salzburg and, as a priest, had conducted his first mass on 15 October 1769. A.M. and L.M. played in the orchestra. The collection was 656 florins (41).

Extract from Hagenauer's calendar, 15 October 1769:
"The mass followed music for the mass composed by Dom Wolfgananus fourteen years of age, which in everyone's opinion was most elegant; the offertory amounted to 656 florins ... then Dom M. played on the great organ for half an hour to the astonishment of all."

K67   CHURCH SONATA IN E FLAT.   Scored for 2 violin: bass: organ. Written in Salzburg in 1772 (3).

K68   CHURCH SONATA IN B FLAT.   Scored for 2 violin: bass: organ. Written in Salzburg, 1772 (2).

K69   CHURCH SONATA IN D MAJOR.   Scored for 2 violin: bass: organ. Written in Salzburg in 1772 (2).

K70   RECITATIVE AND ARIA FOR SOPRANO IN A MAJOR, *A Berenice.* Scored for 2 oboe: 2 horn: strings. Written in Salzburg in December 1766 and first performed on 28 February 1767 in Vologeso, near Salzburg, to celebrate Archbishop Schrattenbach's birthday (see also K36) (11).

K71 ARIA FOR TENOR, *Ah Piu Tremar.*   Scored for 2 oboe: 2 horn: strings. Written in Salzburg in late 1769–early 1770. Words by Metastasio. Only 48 bars are known to exist.

K72 OFFERTORY IN G MAJOR, *Inter Natos Mulierum.*   Scored for S: A: T: B: 2 violin: bass: organ. Written in Salzburg in May and June 1771 for the feast of John the Baptist and performed on 24 June 1771 (5).

K73 SYMPHONY NO 9 IN C MAJOR in four movements.   Scored for 2 oboe/flute: 2 horn: 2 trumpet: timpani: strings. Written in Salzburg in early summer 1772 (12).

K74 SYMPHONY NO 10 IN G MAJOR in three movements.   Scored for 2 oboe: 2 horn: strings. Written in Milan in 1770 (8).

K75 SYMPHONY NO 42 IN F MAJOR in four movements.   Scored for 2 oboe: 2 horn: strings. Written in Salzburg in 1771.

K76 SYMPHONY NO 43 IN F MAJOR in four movements.   Scored for 2 oboe: 2 bassoon: 2 horn: strings. Written in Vienna in 1767. Both these symphonies dubious.

K77 RECITATIVE AND ARIA FOR SOPRANO, *Misero Me.*   Scored for solo S: 2 oboe: 2 bassoon: 2 horn: strings. Words by Mestastasio. Written in Milan, March 1770, together with K88 as a test piece, proving his ability to write opera for the carnival season in December 1770 (see K87) (14).

K78 ARIA FOR SOPRANO, *Per Pieta, Bell, Idol Mio.*   Scored for solo S: 2 oboe: 2 horn: strings. Words by Metasio. Written in 1766 (4).

K79 RECITATIVE AND ARIA FOR SOPRANO, *O Temerario Arbace.*   Scored solo S: 2 oboe: 2 bassoon: 2 horn: strings. Written in 1766 (6).

K80 STRING QUARTET IN G MAJOR.   A.M.'s first string quartet, written on the evening 15 March 1770 in the Inn at Lodi, en route to Bologna. In three movements with a rondo added in 1773 or 1774. Influenced by Sammartini (16).

Extract letter 299, A.M. to L.M., Paris, 24 March 1778:
> *"... before leaving Mannheim I had copies made for Herr von Gemmingen of the quartet which I composed one evening at the Inn at Lodi."* [The last string quartet, K590, was written in June 1790; there are 27 string quartets in all.]

K81   SYMPHONY NO 44 IN D MAJOR in three movements.   Scored for 2 oboe: 2 horn: strings. Written in Rome in April 1770; K95 and K97 were also written the same month, partly by L.M.

Extract letter 89, A.M. to N.M., Rome, 25 April 1770:
> *"... when I have finished this letter I shall write a symphony which I have begun. The aria [K82] is finished."*

K82   ARIA FOR SOPRANO, *Se Ardire, E Speranza.*   Scored for 2 horn: 2 flute: strings. Written in Rome in April 1770, text from Metastasio (5).

Extract letter 88, A.M. to N.M., Rome, 21 April 1770:
> *"Please try to find the arithmetical tables ... I have lost my copy ... so I beg you to copy them out for me with some other examples in arithmetic, and send them to me here."* A.M. loved figures and mental arithmetic.

K83   ARIA FOR SOPRANO, *Se Tutti I Mali Miei.*   Scored for solo S: 2 oboe: 2 horn: strings. Written in Rome in April 1770. There are two versions of this aria (7).

K84   SYMPHONY NO 11 IN D MAJOR in three movements.   Scored for 2 oboe: 2 horn: strings. Written in the summer 1770, but part attributed to L.M.

Extract letter 106, A.M. to N.M., Bologna, 4 August 1770: postscript
> *"It is impossible for me to write a better hand for the pen is for writing music, not for letters. My fiddle has now been restrung and I play every day. But I add this simply because Mama wanted to know where I still play the fiddle ... in the mean time I have composed four Italian symphonies* [K81, K84, K95, K97] *to say nothing of arias of which I must have composed at least five."*

Pope Clement XIV awarded A.M. the high rank of "Knight of the Golden Order". This, a Golden Cross on a red sash, sword and spurs, was presented to him on 8 July 1770. This was in effect a knighthood entitling him to style himself "Signor Cavaliere", but he rarely used this title, as an adult.

Extract letter 102, L.M. to wife, 7 July 1770, Rome:

> *"What I wrote the other day about the cross of an order is quite correct. It is the same order as Gluck's, and is worded as follows ... te creamus ouratae militiae equitem* [we create you a knight of the Golden Cross]*".*

A.M. adds a postscript of letter 102 to N.M:

> *"My compliments to all my good friends. I kiss Mama's hand ... keep well and shit in your bed make a mess of it."* [See K231, Tourette syndrome.]

K85 MISERERE IN A MINOR (psalm 51). Scored for solo treble: A: T: B: bass. Written in Rome 11–14 April 1770.

They arrived in Rome mid-day on Ash Wednesday 11 April 1770, and in the afternoon went to the Sistine Chapel in St Peter's to hear the miserere. This music was considered so beautiful that it was in the Pope's personal possession and only sung on Ash Wednesday, excommunication being at one time the punishment for the infringement of this monopoly. The original was written by Allegri (1582–1652).

Extract letter 87, L.M. to wife, 14 April 1770:

> *"You have often heard of the famous Miserere in Rome which is so greatly prized that the performers are forbidden on pain of excommunication to take away a single part of it, to copy it or to give it to anyone. But we have it already. Wolfgang has written it down perfectly from memory."*

On April 20th A.M. gave a concert in Rome attended by Bonny Prince Charlie (the Young Pretender), who was living in Rome as The Earl of Albany.

Whilst in Rome A.M. met Thomas Linley (1756–1778). Both boys were aged fourteen and child prodigies. Linley was a brilliant violin player and was studying the instrument with Nardini. He began a most promising career as a violinist and composer in Bath and London which was tragically cut short when he drowned in a boating accident whilst on holiday in Lincolnshire.

K86 ANTIPHONE IN D MINOR, *Quaerite Primum.* Scored for choir. Written in Bologna 9 October 1770 for Padre Martini, as part of A.M.'s examination to membership of the Accademia Filarmonica of Bologna (1).

Padre Giovanni Martini (1706–1784) was a Franciscan monk and a composer and teacher; A.M. studied with him whilst in Bologna. His examination for entry was rigorous. Minutes of examination for the Academy:

"Afterwards was read another memorial presented on behalf of Sig. W.A. Mozart of Salzburg, aged fourteen years ... the antiphon was given him to make trial upon; whereupon he, retiring alone, set himself to the task. At the end of less than an hour, the Sig. Mozart completed his trial which, considering the circumstances, was judged to be sufficient ... it was put to the vote ... which when counted was found to be in his favour."

Padre Martini continued to have a great influence on A.M. until his death in 1784. Apart from L.M. he was the only other teacher in his formative years (see K167).

Extract letter 117, L.M. to wife, Bologna, 20 October 1770:

"... all the members of the academy were surprised that Wolfgang had finished his task so quickly, seeing that many candidates had spent three hours over antiphon of three lines. For I must tell you that it is not an easy task, for in this kind of composition many things are not allowed and of these things Wolfgang had been told previously yet he had finished it in less than half and hour."

K87   MITRIDATE.   Opera Seria. Scored for 4 S: A: 2 T: 2 flute: 2 oboe: 2 bass: 4 horn: strings. A.M.'s first opera, written in Milan between August and December 1770, first performance in the Ducal Theatre, Milan, on 26 December 1770 (194).

Extract letter 105, L.M. to wife, Bologna, 28 July 1770:

"... we received yesterday, the libretto and list of singers. The title of this opera will be "Mitridate, Re dei Ponto".

Extract letter 127, L.M. to wife, Milan, 27 December 1770:

"God be praised, the first performance of the opera took place yesterday and won general applause; and two things which have never happened before, occurred on that evening, first an aria of the prima donna was repeated ... secondly, after almost all the arias there was an extraordinary applause and cries of 'evviva il maestro' ... we have christened our son Il Signor Cavaliere Philarmonica."

The first performance on 26 December had 22 consecutive repeats. A.M. conducting the first three from the harpsichord. It lasted for six hours with dinner intervals.

A critic, 2 January 1771:

"... has proved to the publishers satisfaction as much for the tasteful stage designs as for the excellence of the music ... The young maestro, who has not yet reached the age of fifteen, studies the beauty of music and exhibits the rarest of musical graces."

The management of the Milan Ducal Theatre following the success of K87 commissioned another opera (see K135).

K88 ARIA FOR SOPRANO, *Fra cento affanni.* Scored 2 oboe: 2 horn: 2 trumpet: strings. Written in the early spring 1770 in Milan and first performed at Count Firman's house on 12 March 1770 (12).

Extract letter 32, L.M. to wife, Milan, 13 March 1770:

"... it was impossible for me to write to you last Saturday because last Wolfgang had to compose for the concert held yesterday at Count Firman's house, three arias and a recitative with violins ... over 150 leading members of the nobility were present."

Firman was the nephew of the former Archbishop of Salzburg (1758–1762). Both were staying with him and received his support.

K89 KYRIE IN G MAJOR. Written in 1772 (5).

K90 KYRIE IN D MINOR. Written in 1772.

K91 KYRIE IN D MAJOR. Written in 1772.

K92 SOLVE REGINA.

K93 PROFUNDIS IN C MINOR (psalm 129). Written in the summer of 1771. Scored for solo S: A: T: B.

K94 MINUET FOR PIANO IN D MAJOR. Written in Salzburg in 1769 (spurious).

K95 SYMPHONY NO 45 IN D MAJOR. Scored for 2 flute: 2 trumpets: strings. Written in Rome in April 1770.

Extract letter 89, A.M. to N.M., Rome, 25 April 1770:

"When I have finished this letter I shall finish the symphony which I have

begun [K95 or K97] ... *a symphony is being copied, my father is the copyist for we do not wish it to be given out to be copied as it would be stolen ... Tra Liera 25th April 1770, and next year 1771 behind as if in front and double in the middle."*

K96   SYMPHONY NO 46 IN C MAJOR in four movements.   Scored for 2 oboe: 2 horn: 2 trumpet: timpani: strings. Written in Milan in October/November 1771, a minuet added later.

K97   SYMPHONY NO 47 IN D MAJOR in four movements.   Scored for 2 oboe: 2 horn: 2 trumpet: timpani: strings. Written in Rome in April 1770.

K98   SYMPHONY NO 48 IN F MAJOR.

K99   CASSATION IN B FLAT in seven movements.   Scored for 2 oboe: 2 horn: strings. Written in Salzburg in 1769. Cassation, final music, serenade, divertimento are terms used to describe music performed at court functions, theatre or wedding celebrations, often out of doors (17).

K100   SERENADE IN D MAJOR in eight movements.   Scored for 2 oboe/flute: 2 horn: 2 trumpet: strings. Written in Salzburg in 1769 and first performed in honour of the professor of logic at the university, Father Rufinus Widl, on 6 August 1769. A critic wrote "music composed by our most excellent boy, Wolfgang Mozart". (41)

K101   SERENADE IN F MAJOR.   A contredance or country dance written in Salzburg, unknown occasion (6).

K102   SYMPHONY NO 49 IN C MAJOR in one movement.   Used as an overture to *Il Re Pastore* (K208). Scored for 2 flute/oboe: 2 horn: 2 trumpet: strings. Written in Salzburg in the spring of 1775 (8).

K103   MINUETS; 19 in all for orchestra, originally 20.   Scored for 2 oboe/flute: 2 horn/trumpet: strings. Written in Salzburg mid-1772. Dance music.

A.M. was known to love dancing and spent long periods in composing music for the carnival dances which lasted from Epiphany to Shrove Tuesday annually. His output was 195 single dances in total in 25 separate K's.

Towards the end of his life, he is alleged to have remarked when receiving payment for some dance music, *"too much for what I do, too little for what I could do".*

The many dance tunes were published in keyboard arrangements and for string trios to be played in family gatherings. They represent some of the "most infectious, joyous and charming dance music ever written" showing clearly his love of this type of music.

K104   SIX MINUETS FOR ORCHESTRA.   Scored for piccolo: 2 oboe: 2 horn/ trumpet: 2 violin: bass. Written in Salzburg late 1770/early 1771. The first and second minuets arranged from themes provided by Michael Haydn (11).

K105   MINUET FOR ORCHESTRA in six movements.

K106   OVERTURE AND THREE CONTREDANCES.   Scored for 2 oboe: 2 bassoon: 2 horn: 2 violin: bass. Written in Vienna in January 1790 (5).

K107   THREE ARRANGEMENTS after J.C. Bach's original piano scoring. Written in 1771 to be used as show-off pieces whilst touring (32).

K108   REGINA COELI IN C MAJOR.   Scored for solo S: choir: 2 oboe/flute: 2 horn: 2 trumpet: timpani: strings: organ. Written in Salzburg in May 1771, *Regina Coeli* is a psalm sung during mass between Wednesday in Holy Week and Whit Sunday. (See K127 and K276.) (14).

K109   LITANY IN B FLAT, *Lauretannae.*   Scored for solo S: A: T: B: choir: 3 trombones: 2 violin: bass: organ. Written in Salzburg in May 1771 (10).

K110   SYMPHONY NO 12 IN G MAJOR in four movements.   Scored for 2 oboe/flute: 2 bassoon: 2 horn: strings. Written in Salzburg in July 1771 (17).

K111   ASCANIO IN ALBA.   Theatrical serenade. Scored for 4 S: T: choir: 2 flute: 2 oboe/English horn: serpent (a cross between a cornet and a bugle): 2 bassoon: 2 horn: 2 trumpet/horn: timpani: strings. Libretto by Pazini. Commissioned by the Empress Maria Theresia in March 1771 to celebrate the wedding of her son Archduke Ferdinand of Austria and Maria Ricciarda of Moderna, and first performed in the Ducal Theatre on 17 October 1771 (164).

Extract letter 140, L.M. to wife, Milan, 24 August 1771:

> *"I ought to tell you that we have not received from Vienna the text* [of K111] *which everyone is awaiting is with great anxiety, for until it arrives the costumes cannot be made, the stage arrangements nor other details settled."*

Extract letter 146, A.M. to N.M., Milan, 5 October 1771:

> *"Praise and thanks be to God. I too am quite well, but always sleepy ... I have no news except that next Tuesday we shall have another rehearsal* [of K111]*."*

Extract letter 148, L.M. to wife, Milan, 19 October 1771:

> *"... on 17ᵗʰ Wolfgang's serenata, which was such an extraordinary success that it has to be repeated today. The Archduke recently ordered two copies. We are constantly addressed in the street by courtiers and other persons who wish to congratulate the young composer."*

The Archduke wanted to employ A.M. and asked his mother for advice; she writes back to him on 12 December 1771:

> "... you ask me to take the young Salzburger into your service ... I do not know why, not believing that you have need of a composer or of such useless people ... if however it would give you pleasure, I have no wish to hinder you ... only to prevent your burdening yourself with useless people ... if they are in your service it degrades that service when these sort of people go about the world like beggars, besides he has a large family."

The Archduke did not go against his mother, he did not employ A.M.

K112   SYMPHONY NO 13 IN F MAJOR in four movements.   Scored for 2 oboe: 2 horn: strings. Written in Milan 2 November 1771 (16).

K113   DIVERTIMENTO IN E FLAT in four movements.   Scored for 2 clarinet: 2 horn (or English horn): 2 bassoon: strings. Written in Milan in November 1771, using clarinets for the first time. The clarinet became one of A.M.'s favourite instruments. First performed on 22 November 1771 at the house of J.A. Mayr, the imperial paymaster in Milan (15).

K114   SYMPHONY NO 14 IN A MAJOR in four movements.   Scored for 2 flute/oboe: 2 horn: strings. Written in Salzburg 30 December 1771. This is the first of the early *Salzburg Symphonies*, the eight works all being written between the end of 1771 and August 1772. (See K124, K128, K129, K130, K132, K133 and K134.) (22).

K115   SHORT MASS IN C MAJOR.   Scored for S: A: T: B: organ. Partly written in the spring of 1773 but not completed.

K116   SHORT MASS IN F MAJOR.   Scored for S: A: T: B: strings: organ. Only the Kyrie has survived.

K117   OFFERTORY IN C MAJOR, *Benedictus Sit Deus.*   Scored for solo S: choir: 2 flute: 2 horn: 2 trumpet: timpani: strings: organ. Written in Salzburg in 1769 (see K139) (9).

K118   ORATORIO, *La Betulia Libereta.*   Scored for S: T: B: choir: 2 oboe/flute: 2 bassoon: 4 horn: 2 trumpet: strings. Commissioned in Padua and written in the summer of 1771. Libretto by Metastasio.

Extract letter 136, L.M. to wife, Vicenza, 14 March 1771:
> *"... we saw as much of Padua as can be seen in a day and we were not left in peace and Wolfgang had to play at two houses. Moreover he has received a commission to compose an oratorio for Padua which he can do at his leisure."*

Extract letter 516, A.M. to N.M., Vienna, 21 July 1784:
> *"I should be delighted if my father could send me my old oratorio,* La Betulia Libereta. *I have to compose the same oratorio for the society* [the Vienna Tonkunstlersozietat] *in Vienna and possibly I might make use of some of the bits here and there."*

King Frederick William II of Prussia, purchased the manuscript of K118, K125 and K243 after A.M.'s death, his intermediary being the Prussian ambassador in Vienna. The fee paid to the estate was 100 ducats, the date of purchase 18 February 1792. Constanze, A.M.'s widow, sold a number of original manuscripts, and promoted his music extensively after his death. Her second husband, Georg Nissen (1761–1826) went to Vienna in 1793 as a Danish diplomat. He became friendly with Contsanze in 1797 and married her in 1809. They lived in Copenhagen until 1820 when they moved to Salzburg and began collecting material for Nissen's *Biographie W.A.Mozarts* which he left unfinished; it was completed by Constanze and published in 1828.

K119   ARIA FOR SOPRANO, *Der Leibe Himmlisches Gefuhl* (The Heavenly Feeling of Love).   Scored 2 oboe: 2 horn: strings. Written in Vienna in 1782, but now only survives in keyboard form (6).

K120   SYMPHONY NO 50 IN D MAJOR in one movement.   Scored for
2 flute: 2 oboe: 2 horn: 2 trumpet: strings. Written in Milan October/
November 1771 as a finale to be added to the overture to K111 (6).

K121   SYMPHONY IN D MAJOR in one movement, not numbered in
Breitkopf.   Scored for 2 oboe: 2 horn: strings. Written in Salzburg end
of 1774 as a finale to be added to the overture to *La Finta Giardiniera*
(K196) (7).

K122   MINUET FOR ORCHESTRA IN E FLAT.   Scored for 2 oboe: 2 horn:
2 violin: bass. Written in Bologna in August 1770. On the back of this
manuscript L.M. requests that his book *Versuch einer grundlichen Violinschule*
published in 1756 be sent to Padre Martini (1).

Extract letter 116, L.M. to wife, Bologna, 5 October 1770:
> *"Padre Martini has already received my book. We are now the best of*
> *friends. We* [L.M. and A.M.] *are at his house every day and have long*
> *discussions on the history of music."* [See K86.]

K123   CONTRADANCE FOR ORCHESTRA IN B FLAT in one movement.
Scored for 2 oboe: 2 horn: 2 violin: bass. Written in Rome 13–14 April
1770 (2).

Extract letter 87, L.M. to wife, Rome, 14 April 1770:
> *"... today and yesterday I have been a bit of an invalid for I have taken*
> *three digestive powders, but thank God, I feel well. Wolfgang is splendid and*
> *sends herewith a contradance* [K123]. *He would like Herr Hofmand to make*
> *up steps for it; when two violins play as leaders, only two persons should*
> *lead the dance; but whenever the orchestra comes in with all the*
> *instruments, the whole company should dance together."*

K124   SYMPHONY NO 15 IN G MAJOR in four movements.   Scored for
2 oboe: 2 horn: strings. Written in Salzburg 21 February 1772 (see
K114) (16).

K125   LITANY IN B FLAT, *Litanie De Venerabili Altaris Sacramento.*   Scored
for solo S: A: T: B: choir: 2 oboe/flute: 2 trumpet: strings: organ. Written in
Salzburg in March 1772, modelled on L.M.'s outlined work, but expanded and
surpassed it, and with A.M. playing the violin, performed in the Hour Service
on New Year's Day 1775 in Munich (42).

Extract letter 190, L.M. to wife, Munich, 14 December 1774:

"Then you will find Wolfgang's great Litany. The score is with it, bound in blue paper. Make quite sure that all the parts are there, the two litanies are to be performed here in the Hours on New Year's Day."

K126   SCIPIO'S DREAM.   Festival opera. Scored for 2 S: 3 T: 2 flute: 2 oboe: 2 bassoon: 2 horn: 2 trumpet: timpani: strings. Libretto by Metastasio. This festival opera commissioned to celebrate the new Archbishop of Salzburg's installation on 29 April 1772, in the Archbishop's Palace (112).

This work was originally dedicated to the previous Archbishop of Salzburg, Schrattenbach, who died on 16 December 1771. On 14 March 1772 Hieronymus Colloredo was elected Prince-Archbishop of Salzburg. The new Archbishop treated A.M. like a servant, refused him time off for touring; A.M.'s dislike of him eventually contributed to his leaving Salzburg for good in 1781. He was paid 150 florins annually.

K127   REGINA COELI IN B FLAT.   Scored for solo S: choir: 2 oboe/flute: 2 horn: strings: organ. Written in Salzburg in May 1772 as a small gift to Joseph Haydn's wife. (She was a most unsatisfactory woman for Haydn, they lived apart a lot of the time.) (15).

K128   SYMPHONY NO 16 IN C MAJOR in three movements.   Scored for 2 oboe: 2 horn: strings. Written in Salzburg in May 1772 (14).

K129   SYMPHONY NO 17 IN G MAJOR in three movements.   Scored for 2 oboe: 2 horn: strings. Written in Salzburg in May 1772 (17).

K130   SYMPHONY NO 18 IN F MAJOR in four movements.   Scored for 2 flute: 4 horn: strings. Written in Salzburg in May 1772 (22).   *age 16*

K131   DIVERTIMENTO IN D MAJOR in seven movements.   Scored for flute: oboe: bassoon: 4 horn: strings. Written in Salzburg in June 1772, more in a serenade form (31).

K132   SYMPHONY NO 19 IN E FLAT in four movements.   Scored for 2 oboe: 4 horn: strings. Written in Salzburg in July 1772 (23).

K133   SYMPHONY NO 20 IN D MAJOR in four movements.   Scored for flute: 2 oboe: 2 horn: 2 trumpet: strings. Written in Salzburg in July 1772 (29).

K134   SYMPHONY NO 21 IN A MAJOR in four movements.   Scored for
2 flute: 2 horn: strings. Written in Salzburg August 1772, the last of the
Salzburg Symphonies of 1772 (20).

K135   LUCIO SILLA.   Opera Seria. Scored for 4 S: 2 T: choir: 2 oboe/flute:
2 bassoon: 2 horn: 2 trumpet: timpani: strings. Written in Salzburg and Milan.
First performed in Milan on 26 December 1772 in the Regio Ducal Theatre for
the carnival season. Libretto by Giovanni di Gamerra (212).

Performed 26 times during the carnival of 1772/3, the first performance at 8
instead of 6 o'clock because the Archduke Ferdinande was delayed on official
business; lasted till 2am with long dinner interval. The fee was 130 gulden
and furnished lodgings whilst in Milan. Aloisia Webber sang 2 arias in this
opera; A.M. fell in love with her but she rejected him. There were four
Webber daughters; A.M. eventually married Constanze, whose voice was
inferior to Aloisia.

Extract letter 161, L.M. to wife, Milan, 14 November 1772:
> *"Not one of the singers has arrived yet except Signora Suarti, who sings the
> part of Secondo Uomo ... Wolfgang has got much amusement from
> composing the choruses of which there are to be three and from acting and
> partly re-writing the few recitations which he composed in Salzburg."*

Extract letter 166, A.M. to N.M., Milan, 18 December, 1772:
> *"I hope you are well, my dear sister. When you receive this letter my dear
> sister, that very evening my opera will have been performed, my dear sister.
> Think of me, my dear sister, and try as hard as you can to imagine that you,
> my dear sister, are hearing it and seeing it too, my dear sister. Go and shit
> in your bed."*

Extract letter 167, L.M. to wife, Milan, 26 December, 1772:
> *"The opera is to begin in about two or three hours. May God be
> gracious ..."*

Extract letter 168, L.M. to wife, Milan, 2 January 1773:
> *"The opera was a great success ... picture to yourself the whole theatre,
> which by half past five was so full that not any other soul could get in. On
> the first evening the singers and we are always very nervous."*

K136   DIVERTIMENTO STRING QUARTET IN D MAJOR.   Written in early
1772 (12).

-56

age 16

K137   DIVERTIMENTO STRING QUARTET IN B FLAT.   Written in early 1772 (11).

K138   DIVERTIMENTO STRING QUARTET IN F MAJOR.   Written in early 1772. These three divertimento all have three movements, and no minuets, so are not therefore correctly divertimento. They were written in preparation for his third and last Italian tour (24 October 1772–13 March 1773). He added wind instruments if the players were available (12).

K139   MASS IN C MINOR.   Scored for solo S: A: T: B: choir: 2 oboe: 4 trumpets: 3 trombone: timpani: strings: organ. Written in Vienna in the autumn of 1768, and first performed in the recently built church of Father Parhammer's orphanage in Vienna on 7 December 1768 (45).

Extract letter 67, L.M. to Hagenauer, Vienna, 12 November 1768:
"… the new church of Father Parhammer's orphanage will be blessed on the Feast of the Immaculate Conception. For this feast, Wolfgang has composed a solemn mass [K139], an offertorium [K117] and a trumpet concerto for a boy [this has been lost] and has dedicated them to the orphanage. Presumably Wolfgang himself will conduct this music."

From a newspaper report:
"His Imperial and Royal Majesty was graciously pleased to visit the orphanage on the Rennweg, to be present at the first solemn consecration and service of the newly built church … the whole of the music for the orphan's choir at high mass has been composed throughout for this solemnity by Wolfgang Mozart the little son aged 12 (but already well known for his talents) … performed by himself to general applause and admiration, with the greatest accuracy; and apart from all this he also sang in the motets." [His singing voice was thin and small.]

K140   SHORT MASS IN G MAJOR.   Scored for solo S: A: T: B: choir: 2 violin: bass. Written in Salzburg in 1773 but no definite autograph; doubtful (16).

K141   TE DEUM IN C MAJOR.   Scored for choir: 4 trumpet: timpani: 2 violin: bass: organ. Written in Salzburg in 1769, closely modelled on the *Te Deum* by Michael Haydn as a technical exercise, "but still Mozartean in flavour" (7).

K142   TANTUM ERGO IN B FLAT.   Unlikely to be by A.M., possibly J. Zach (5).

K143   ARIA FOR SOPRANO IN G MAJOR, *Ergo Interest.* A motet.   Scored for solo S: strings: organ. Written in Salzburg in late 1773 (5).

K144   CHURCH SONATA IN D MAJOR.   Scored for 2 violin: bass: organ. Written in Salzburg in 1774 (2).

K145   CHURCH SONATA IN F MAJOR.   Scored for 2 violin: bass: organ. Written in Salzburg in 1774 (2).

K146   ARIA FOR SOPRANO IN B FLAT, *Commer Hur.*   Scored for solo S: strings: organ. Written in Salzburg in March/April 1779 (5).

K147   SONG IN F MAJOR, *Wie Unglucklich Bin Ich Nit.*   Piano accompaniment written in Salzburg in 1775 or 1776 (1)

K148   SONG IN D MAJOR, *Lobegesang Auf Die Feirliche.*   Words by L.F. Lenz. Written in Salzburg in 1775/6 as a Masonic song (2).

K149   SONG, *Ich Hab Es Langst.*   Text by Gunther. Influenced by Phillip Emmanuel Bach, who was a good friend of L.M. and this is possibly by the father.

K150   SONG, *Was Ich In Gedanken Kusse* (What I kiss in my thoughts).

K151   SONG, *Ich Trachte Nicht* (Contentment I Strove Not).   Words by Canitz.

K152   CANZONETTA.   An arrangement either by L.M. or A.M. from an aria by Mysluiecek (Canzonetta means a light, flowing song).

K153   FUGUE FOR PIANO IN E FLAT.   Written in Salzburg in 1783, not complete and finished by S.Sechter.

K154   FUGUE FOR PIANO IN G MINOR.   Written in Vienna in 1782, not complete.

K155 STRING QUARTET IN D MAJOR.   Written on the third Italian journey en route to Milan in October/early November 1772. Influenced by Sammartini, in the Italian style (10).

Extract letter 159, L.M. to wife, Bozen, 18 October 1772:
> *"Wolfgang is well too and at the moment is writing a quartet* [K155] *to while away the time. He sends greetings to everyone."*

Postscript by A.M. to N.M., same letter:
> *"We have already reached Bozen. Already? I mean at last. I am hungry, thirsty, sleepy and lazy but I feel well!"*

K156 STRING QUARTET IN G MAJOR.   Written in Milan at the end of 1772, showing the influence of early Haydn (14).

K157 STRING QUARTET IN C MAJOR.   Written in Milan end of 1772/early 1773 (11).

Extract letter 175, L.M. to wife, Milan, 6 February 1773:
> *"We have no means of heating our room, not even a fireplace, I can only try to keep myself warm in a bed covered with fur and clothes ... Wolfgang is composing a quartet, and I am relieved that I have written this letter. We kiss you many hundred, million times and I am your own disabled M.L.T."*

K158 STRING QUARTET IN F MAJOR.   Written in Milan end 1772/early 1773 (16).

K159 STRING QUARTET IN B FLAT.   Written in Milan early 1773 (13).

K160 STRING QUARTET IN E FLAT.   Written in Milan early in 1773 (11) These six quartets K155–K160 are known as the *Italian Quartets* and all were influenced by G.B. Sammartini (1698–1775) organist at Milan cathedral.

K161 SYMPHONY IN D MAJOR (no Breitkopf number) in three movements. Scored for 2 flute: 2 oboe: 2 horn: 2 trumpet: timpani: strings. Written in Salzburg in 1773 or 1774. Two movements taken from the overture to the opera K126 *Scipio's Dream* (8).

K162 SYMPHONY NO 22 IN C MAJOR in three movements.   Scored for 2 oboe: 2 horn: 2 trumpet: strings. Written in Salzburg 19 or 29 April 1773, the autograph showing both dates (10).

On 22 May 1987, at Sotheby's auction house in London, K162, K181, K182, K183, K184, K199, K200, K201 and K202 were sold at auction for £2,585,000. They were bound together in one volume of 508 pages in A.M.'s own hand, autographed primary source (this is the definitive undisputed score). This is a description of the manuscript from the Sotheby's catalogue:

> "Lot no. 457 (1) Symphony no. 22 in C Major K162. In three separate movements, with autographed title *Sinfia di Wolgango Amadeo Mozart.* The date heavily deleted, see above, marked no.1 in another hand on the first page in brown crayon, notated in brown ink, mostly on eight staves per page, some staves extended into the margin by the composer. Scored for 2 oboe: 2 horn: 2 'trombe lunghe' and strings, a working manuscript in places, with deletion of four bars on page 11 and two bars on page 25 and a number of corrections and alterations, marked by the printer in pencil. 40 pages, in good condition, a little staining."

K163   SYMPHONY IN D MAJOR, the finale of K161. This movement added to the overture K126, see above. Written in 1773.

K164   SIX MINUETS FOR ORCHESTRA, the first 3 in D major, last three in G major.   Scored for flute: oboe: horn/trumpet: 2 violin: bass. Written in Salzburg in June 1772 (12).

K165   MOTET FOR SOPRANO IN F MAJOR, *Exultate Jubilate.*   Scored for solo S: 2 oboe: 2 horn: strings: organ. Written in Milan in January 1773 for the Castrato Venanzio Rauzzini (the last major castrato, as in the early 1770's this practice became illegal). First performed by him on 17 January 1773 in the Theatinene Church, Milan (17).

Extract letter 170a, A.M. to N.M., Milan, 16 January 1773:

> *"I for have the primo a nomo motet composed* [K165] *which to tomorrow at church the theatine performed be will. Keep well I beg you. Farewell, addio. I sorry to any my to our friends, I am not have news."*

From a newspaper report:

> "On 17th January 1773 the new motet *Exultate Jubilate* [K165] was sung by Venanzio Rauzzine castrato, at the Theatine in Milan. Virtuoso work for solo soprana and lavish orchestral accompaniment and concluding with the Alleluia."

This is one of the most famous non operatic arias of the period and remains so today, as one of Mozart's "best pieces" Italian vocal works. L.M. was ill but this piece was composed to show A.M.'s ability and his eligibility for a permanent position in the flourishing Italian music scene of the period, but alas without any success. Revised in Salzburg in October 1773.

The *Exultate Jubilate* is sung during the mass after the Credo.

K166 DIVERTIMENTO IN E FLAT.   Scored for 2 oboe: 2 clarinet: 2 English horn: 2 horn: 2 bassoon. Written in Salzburg 24 March 1773 (13).

K167 MASS IN C MAJOR, *Holy Trinity.*   Scored for choir: 2 oboe: 4 trumpet (or 3 trombone): timpani: 2 violin: bass: organ. Written in Salzburg in June 1773 for Archbishop Colloredo who liked short masses and was impatient to get the service over as quickly as possible (never more than 45 minutes), hence no soloists (25).

Extract letter 205, A.M. to Padre Martini, Salzburg, 4 September 1776:
"Our church music is very different to that of Italy, since a mass with the whole Kyrie , the Gloria, the Credo, the Epistle, the Offertory or Motet, the Sanctus and the Agnus Dei, must not last longer than three quarters of an hour. This applies even to the most solemn mass said by the Archbishop himself. So you see that a special study is required for this composition. At the same time, the mass must have all the instruments, trumpets, drums and so forth … I never cease to grieve that I am far away from that one person in the world that I love, revere and esteem most of all and whose most humble and devoted servant, Most Reverant Father I shall always be. W.A.M."

K168 STRING QUARTET IN F MAJOR (15).

K169 STRING QUARTET IN A MAJOR (16).

K170 STRING QUARTET IN C MAJOR (17).

K171 STRING QUARTET IN E FLAT (8).

K172 STRING QUARTET IN B FLAT (16).

K173 STRING QUARTET IN D MINOR (18).

The first four of these string quartets, known as the *Viennese Quartets,* were written together in August 1773, and the last two in September 1773. All were influenced by the recently published string quartets, opus 20, of Joseph Haydn.

These six string quartets are not to be confused with either the Italian quartets (K155–K160), see above, or the later six Haydn quartets of 1785 (see K387, K421, K428, K458, K464 and K465). These six quartets were advertised by the publisher Artaria in September 1785 and were confused with the new Haydn quartets that were published at the same time. A.M. published an apology for this confusion:

> *"Herr Mozart regards it as his duty to inform the estimable public that the six quartets are by no means new, but an old, written by him as long ago as fifteen years* [incorrect, it was twelve years, in 1773] *so that amateurs who had been expecting the new ones should not be wrongly served."*

This newspaper apology for the mistake raises the exploitation of composers' works and the difficulties encountered in gaining a fair income from compositions when no copyright advantages existed, and there was no possibility of stopping publishers from advertising new work without any benefit to the composer. A.M. was the last of the generation to be tied to a generous benefactor, but also the first genuinely to "go it alone" with various degrees of success. In his early years in Vienna from 1781 to 1785 he achieved very considerable success, promoting profitably his own concerts, teaching and composing, whereas after 1785 the gloss seems to have gone off the public's fascination with him as a performer and as a "wonder-child", hence his increasing indebtedness to others.

K174 STRING QUINTET IN B FLAT. A.M.'s first quintet, started early in 1773 and completed with some revision at the end of that year in Salzburg, under the influence of Michael Haydn. Boccherini (1743–1805) cannot have been unknown to A.M. as his string quintets were becoming famous at the same time (27).

K175 PIANO CONCERTO NO 5 IN D MAJOR in three movements. Scored for solo piano: 2 oboe: 2 horn: 2 trumpet: timpani: strings. Written in Salzburg in December 1773 as the first "true piano concerto". Written originally for the harpsichord. A new finale was added to this concerto in March 1782 (see K382) (23).

Extract letter 286a, A.M. to L.M., Mannheim, 14 February 1778:

> *"... yesterday there was a concert Cannabich's where all the music was my*
> *own composition ... then I played my old concerto in D major* [K175]
> *because it is such a favourite here, and then I also extemporized for half and*
> *hour."*

K176   SIXTEEN MINUETS FOR ORCHESTRA: (1) C Major; (2) G Major; (3)
E Flat; (4) B Flat; (5) F Major; (6) D Major; (7) A Major; (8) C Major; (9)
G Major; (10) B Flat; (11) F Major; (12) D Major; (13) G Major; (14) C Major;
(15) F Major; (16) D Major.   All scored for 2 oboe/flute: 2 bassoon:
2 horn/trumpet: 2 violin: bass. Written in December 1773 (30).

K177   OFFERTORY, *Sub Exposito Venerabili.* Spurious, possibly by L.M.

K178   ARIA FOR SOPRANO, *Ah Spiegarti Oh Dio.*   Accompaniment only
surviving in piano form. Revised K418. Written in Vienna in June 1783 (4).

K179   VARIATION FOR PIANO IN C MAJOR.   Scored for solo piano. Written
in Salzburg in the summer of 1774. Variations from the finale of an oboe
concerto by J.C. Fischer and used by A.M. as a virtuoso piano display piece (14).

Played by A.M. at a concert on 22 October 1777 in the Fugger Concert Hall in
Augsburg: entrance fee 1 florin; A.M. earned 83.5 florins. An announcement
of this concert:

> "... to have a composer, a compatriot [L.M. was born in Augsburg, baptised
> on 14 November 1719 in St George, Augsburg], here with us whom the
> whole of England, France and Italy envies us ... will be aware this can be
> nobody else than A.M. who did such great wonders before in his tender
> youth. Let us see whether he will do it for us again too. Tomorrow,
> Wednesday 22nd October, Chevalier Mozart will hold a concert in the
> Fugger Hall ... where to defray the costs one florin for the first place and 30
> kreuzer for the second which will be paid immediately on admission."

Critic from the local newspaper, 28 October 1777:

> "... one found here mastery in the thought, mastery in the performance,
> the melody so agreeable, so playful ... the rendering on the fortepiano so
> neat, so clean, so full of expression and yet at the same time
> extraordinarily rapid, so that one hardly knew what to give attention to
> first, and all the hearers were enraptured ... had a especial satisfaction of
> concluding from the stillness and general applause that we have here to

appreciate true beauty ... to hear a virtuoso who may place himself side by side with the great masters of our nation, and yet is at least half our own."

This is a clear indication that as a performer A.M. had no equal, and K179 was a perfect piece with which to shine and show off pianistic skills (Beethoven, Chopin and Listz had their own demonstration pieces).

K180   VARIATIONS FOR PIANO IN G MAJOR.   Scored for solo piano. Written in Vienna in the autumn of 1773. Variations from an opera by Salieri (6).

Extract letter 344, L.M. to A.M., Salzburg, 10 December 1778:
> *"I have already set up music engraving here, as I have found someone who I have trained. On your arrival you will find here your variations on Saliere arioso* [K180] *engraved on seven sheets. I only wish you had not made them so well known, for then I could sell more copies."*

K181   SYMPHONY NO 23 IN D MAJOR in three movements.   Scored for 2 oboe: 2 horn: 2 trumpet: strings. Written in Salzburg on 19 May 1773 (8).

Sotheby's catalogue:
> "... in three continuous movements with autograph title *Sinfonia di Wolfgango Mozart*, the date heavily deleted marked no.2 in another page on the first page in brown crayon, notated in brown ink, mostly on eight staves per page,   Scored for 2 oboes, 2 horns, 2 clarini and strings, including 2 violas, some corrections and alterations; 47 pages with the forty-eighth page blank. Fols. 2 and 3 detached, a little staining."

K182   SYMPHONY NO 24 IN F FLAT in three movements.   Scored for 2 oboe/flute: 2 horn: strings. Written in Salzburg 3 October 1773 (9).

Sotheby's catalogue:
> "Symphony no 24 in B flat major in three separate movements with autograph title *Sinfonia Del Sgr Cavaliere Wolfgango Amadeo Mozart*, the words *del sgr Cavaliere* probably in the hand of Leopold the dated heavily deleted marked no.3 in another hand on the first page in brown crayon, notated in brown ink, mostly on eight staves per page, scored for 2 oboes (replaced by 2 flutes in the Andantino grazioso), 2 horns and strings, some deletions and alterations, foliated in pencil in another hand, forty pages."

K183   SYMPHONY NO 25 IN G MINOR in four movements.   Scored for
2 oboe: 2 bassoon: 4 horn: strings. Written in Salzburg 5 October 1773, the
first movement in a minor key associated with K550 in G minor, 15 years
later (28).

17

Sotheby's catalogue:
"… no. 25 in G minor, the first of Mozart's two great symphonies in
G minor, one of the composer's most telling keys; in four separate
movements without title, inscribed by *Leopold Mozart Del Sgr Cavialiere
Amadeo Wolfgango Mozart*, the date heavily deleted, too annotations by
Leopold on the last page marked no.4 in another hand on the first page in
brown crayon, a few light annotations by the printer in pencil, the
remainder of the manuscript entirely autograph, notated in brown ink on
up to nine staves per page,   Scored for 2 oboes, 4 horns and strings, 2
bassoons replacing 2 horns in the slow movements and in the Trio; A
working manuscript in places, with a number of alterations, corrections
and deletions, including two whole bars deleted on page 10, and three bars
at the beginning of the slow movement (in effect a false start). Seventy-six
pages."

K184   SYMPHONY NO 26 IN E FLAT in three movements.   Scored for
2 flute: 2 oboe: 2 bassoon: 2 horn: 2 trumpet: strings. Written in Salzburg
30 March 1773 (19).

Sotheby's catalogue:
"Symphony No.26 in E flat Major. In three continuous movements, the first
two pages of the first movement in the hand of Leopold Mozart, the
remainder of the movement, i.e. page three to page twenty-one in the hand
of a copyist, the second and third movements, i.e. page twenty-one to
forty-eight in the hand of Wolfgang Amadeus without title, inscribed by
Leopold *Del Sgr. Cavaliere Amadeo Mozart*, the date heavily deleted
marked no5 in another hand on the first page in brown crayon, notated
in brown ink on up to ten staves per page,   Scored for 2 flutes, 2 oboes,
2 horns, 2 trumpets, 2 bassoon and strings, including 2 violas, with a
number of corrections and alterations forty-eight pages."

K185   SERENADE IN D MAJOR in seven movements, known as the
Andretter Serenade.   Scored for 2 oboe/flute: 2 horn: 2 trumpet: solo violin.
Written in Vienna in July 1773 and first performed on 1 August 1773 for the
wedding reception of the oldest son of Johann Andretter, the military

councillor to the Salzburg court. Played also at the Salzburg University as finale music at the end of term party (46).

K186   DIVERTIMENTO IN B FLAT.   Scored for 2 oboe: 2 clarinet: 2 English horn: 2 horn: 2 bassoon. Written in Milan in March 1773 (the clarinet was a new instrument and was not available in Austria until 1771) (12).

K187   DIVERTIMENTO IN C MAJOR.   Eight short pieces. Scored for 2 flute: 5 trumpet: 4 timpani. Written in Salzburg in 1773 for the Salzburg Cavalry riding school summer festival.

K188   DIVERTIMENTO IN C MAJOR.   Six short pieces. Scored for 2 flute: 5 trumpet: 4 timpani. Written together with K187 for the same festival (10).

K189   MARCH IN D MAJOR.   Scored for 2 flute: 2 horn: 2 trumpet: 2 violins: bass. Written in Vienna in July/August 1773 also for the end of term festivities (5).

K190   CONCERTONE IN C MAJOR.   Scored for 2 violins: solo oboe: cello: 2 oboe: 2 horn: 2 trumpet: strings. Written in Salzburg 31 May 1774, why and for whom not known (22).

Extract letter 260, A.M. to L.M., Mannheim, 14 December 1777:

> *"I played through my concertone* [K190] *to Herr Wenlding on the claviere. He remembered that it was just the thing for Paris. When I play it to Baron Bagge he is quite beside himself. Adieu."*

Baron Bagge was famous for his musical salons and was a great supporter of A.M. and his mother whilst in Paris.

K191   CONCERTO FOR BASSOON IN B FLAT.   Scored for solo bassoon: 2 oboe: 2 horn: strings. Written in Salzburg 4 June 1774. Why or for whom not known (19).

K192   SHORT MASS IN F MAJOR, *The Little Credo.*   Scored for solo S: A: T: B: choir: 2 trumpet or 3 trombone: 2 violin: bass: organ. Written in Salzburg 14 June 1774 for Archbishop, Count Colloredo. (Note that the credo melody was used in the *Jupiter Symphony*, see K551.) (25).

Extract letter 201, L.M. to wife, Munich, 15 February 1775:

"Thank God, all three of us are well, but I shall be glad when this carnival is over. We shall probably travel home on Ash Wednesday. The short mass [K192] by Wolfgang was performed last Sunday in the court chapel and I conducted it. Next Sunday another mass [K167, Holy Trinity] is to be performed. Yesterday we had extraordinary weather just like April, now fine, nor raining."

K193   DIXITE AND MAGNIFICAT IN C MAJOR.   Scored for solo S: T: choir: 2 trumpet: 3 trombone: 2 violin: bass. Written in Salzburg in July 1774 (17).

K194   SHORT MASS IN D MAJOR.   Scored for solo S: A: T: B: choir: 3 trombone: 2 violin: bass: organ. Written in Salzburg 8 August 1774, being influenced by Joseph Haydn's *Missa St Nicholai* (22).

K195   LITANY, *Larettine In D Major.*   Scored for solo S: A: T: B: choir: 2 oboe: 2 horn or 3 trombone: strings: organ. Written in Salzburg in April/May 1774 to be performed in Salzburg Cathedral (31).

K196   LA FINTA GIARDINIERA, opera buffa (The Make-Believe Garden Girl).   Scored for 4 S: 2: B: 2 flute: 2 oboe: 2 bassoon: 2 horn: 2 trumpet: English horn: timpani: strings. Written at the end of 1774 early 1775 with its first performance in the Munich Assembly Rooms on 13 January 1775 (150).

Extract letter 196, A.M. to mother, Munich, 11 January 1775:

"Thank God all three of us are quite well. It is impossible for me to write a long letter, as I am off this very moment to a rehearsal of my opera. Tomorrow we are having a dress rehearsal and the performance takes place on Friday 13th. Mamma must not worry it will go off quite well."

Extract letter 197, A.M. to mother, Munich, 14 January 1775:

"Thank God, my opera was performed yesterday, 13th, for the first time and was such a success that it is impossible for me to describe to Mamma. In the first place the whole theatre was so packed that a great many people were turned away ... then after each aria there was terrific noise, clapping of hands and cries of Viva Maestro."

It was performed twice only again in his lifetime. A critic wrote after the second performance:

"On Friday Their Electorial Highnesses were present at the first performance of the Opera Buffa ... the music was generally applauded; it is by the young Mozart, aged eighteen of Salzburg, who is here at the moment. He is the same who went to England and elsewhere at the age of eight to be heard on the harpsichord, which he plays superbly well."

A further critic:

"I also heard an Opera Buffa by that wonderful genius, Mozart [K196] flashes of genius appear here and there, but it rises towards Heaven in clouds of incense – a scent beloved of the Gods. If Mozart is not a plant forced in the hot-house he is bound to grow into one of the greatest musical composers who ever lived."

K197   TANTUM ERGO.   Scored for choir: 2 "treble instruments": strings: organ. Written in Salzburg in 1774 but possibly not by A.M. (see also K142 Tantum Ergo) (5).

K198   OFFERTORY IN F MAJOR, *Sub Tuum Praesidium.*   Scored for solo S: T: strings: organ. Written in Salzburg in 1774 (4).

K199   SYMPHONY NO 27 IN G MAJOR in three movements.   Scored for 2 flute: 2 horn: strings. Written in Salzburg in April 1773 (21).

Sotheby's catalogue:

"... in three separate movements, inscribed by Leopold Mozart; *Symphonia Del Sgr. Caval. Amadeo Wolfg (ang). Mozart* The date heavily deleted marked no.6 in another hand on the first page in brown crayon, the remainder entirely autograph, notated in brown ink, mostly on seven staves per page,   Scored for 2 flutes, 2 horns and strings, including 2 violas, some deletions, alterations and corrections, fifty-two pages."

K200   SYMPHONY NO 28 IN C MAJOR in four movements.   Scored for 2 oboe: 2 horn: 2 trumpet: strings. Written in Salzburg 17 November 1773 (26).

Sotheby's catalogue: (this shld. have been dated) → 1987 ?

"... written in Salzburg 17th November 1774, but date not certain, possibly 1773 as the year on the manuscript is illegible. One of the greatest of Mozart's early symphonies in four separate movements with autograph title *Sinfonia Di Wolfgango Amadeo Mozart*, the date heavily deleted, marked number seven in another hand on the first page in brown crayon, notated in brown ink, mostly on eight staves per page,

Scored for 2 oboes, 2 horns, 2 trumpets and strings, some deletions and
alterations, including one bar entirely deleted on page fifty, and
trumpet parts deleted on page sixty-six and page sixty-seven, page
sixty-eight blank, small repair on foot of page ten not effecting the
music."

K201   SYMPHONY NO 29 IN A MAJOR in four movements.   Scored for
2 oboe: 2 horn: strings. Written in Salzburg 6 April 1774 (31).

Sotheby's catalogue:
"One of Mozart's greatest Symphonies, the most important of this group,
the 'crowning achievement of Mozart's symphonies' (Jen's *Peter Larsen
The Symphonies, The Mozart Companion,* ed. H.C. Robbins Landon and
Donald Mitchell, London 1956, page 175). In four separate movements
with autograph title *Sinfonia Wolfgang Amadeo Mozart,* the date heavily
deleted, the words 'six (apri) le ... a salisbrugo' just discernible, marked
number 8 in another hand on the first page in brown crayon, notated in
brown ink, mostly on seven staves per page,   Scored for 2 oboes,
2 horns, and strings, with violas in two parts in places, some deletions,
alterations and corrections, 79 pages (page 80 blank)."

K202   SYMPHONY NO 30 IN D MAJOR in four movements.   Scored for
2 oboe: 2 horn: 2 trumpet: strings. Written in Salzburg 5 May 1774 the last of
nine sold in 1987 (26).

Sotheby's catalogue:
"... in four separate movements, with autograph title ... *Sinfonia di
Wolfgang Amadeo Mozart* the date heavily deleted marked number nine in
another hand on the first page in brown crayon, notated in brown ink,
mostly on eight staves per page,   Scored for 2 oboes, 2 horns, 2 trombe
lunge, strings, with a number of alterations, deletions, and corrections, a
few annotations in pencil and black ink in another hand, 55 pages in all,
the verse of the last folio laid down, folios two and three detached.

Note. The description of each manuscript in the Sotheby's catalogue, Friday
22 May 1987, lot 457, was in the sale of Continental Printed books
manuscripts and music. With their permission. See K162.

K203   SERENADE IN D MAJOR in eight movements.   Scored for
2 oboe/flute: bassoon: 2 horn: 2 trumpet: violin solo: strings. Written in

Salzburg in August 1774 for the Archbishop of Salzburg's name-day (Colloredo), 30 September. Known now as *The Colloredo Serenade* (see K237) (47).

K204   SERENADE IN D MAJOR in seven movements (2 movements added from K121).   Scored for 2 oboe/flute: 1 bassoon: 2 horn: 2 trumpet: solo violin: strings. Written in Salzburg 5 August 1775 and first performed on 9 August 1775 as "Final-musik" at Salzburg university (42).

K205   DIVERTIMENTO IN D MAJOR in five movements.   Scored for 2 horn: bassoon: solo violin: strings. Written in Salzburg in 1773 and first performed in the garden of Dr Mesmer's house in Vienna, in the Landstrasse, at mid-day on 18 August 1773 (23).

Dr Mesmer was a great supporter of A.M. Apart from his quasi-medical practice he had married a rich widow and had a small theatre built in the gardens where many musical concerts took place, among them K205 (see also K50).

K206   MARCH, *Idomeneo.*

K207   VIOLIN CONCERTO IN B FLAT.   Scored for solo violin: 2 oboe: 2 horn: strings. Written in Salzburg 14 April 1775 for A.M. himself to play. Unknown when first performed. A rondo (K269) written in 1776 replaces the original rondo, and was played in this new form by Antonio Brunetti, the Salzburg Concertmaster (leader of the orchestra (20).

Extract letter 331, A.M. to L.M., Paris, 11 September 1778:
> *"… on a journey one needs money. If I have time I shall rearrange some of my violin concertos and shorten them."*

There is some dispute about the date of this first violin concerto. Possibly written in 1773/4, two years ahead of the group K211, K216, K218 and K219, which were all written between June and December 1775 for Brunetti.

K208   IL RE PASTORE (*The Shepherd King*).   A cantate in a semi-staged form. Scored for 3S: 2T: 2 flute: 2 oboe/English horn: 2 bassoon: 2 horn: 2 trumpet/horn: strings. Written in Salzburg early in 1775 and first performed in the Archbishop's Palace on 23 April 1775 to commemorate the visit of Archduke Maximilian Franz, the youngest son of Empress Marie Theresia. Libretto by Metastasio (121).

From the Archduke's journal, Salzburg, 23 April 1775:

"... moreover the evening was again concluded as the day before, with a musique-concert, and supper ... so the music this evening was by no lesser person than the famous Mozart ... the young Mozart was heard on the claviere and played various things by heart with as much art as pleasureness." [See K111 eldest son.]

K209   ARIA FOR TENOR, *Si Mostra La Sorte.*   Scored for solo T: 2 flute: 2 horn: strings. Written in Salzburg 19 May 1775, intended to be inserted into an opera, possibly K208 (3).

K210   ARIA FOR TENOR, *Con Rispetto.*   Scored for solo T: 2oboe: 2 horn: strings. Written in Salzburg in May 1775, as above K209 (3).

K211   VIOLIN CONCERTO IN D MAJOR.   Scored for solo violin: 2 oboe: 2 horn: strings. Written in Salzburg 14 June 1775 again for Brunetti to play (see K207) (27).

K212   CHURCH SONATA IN B FLAT.   Scored for 2 violin: bass: organ. Written in 1775 (2).

K213   DIVERTIMENTO FOR WIND IN F MAJOR.   Scored for 2 oboe: 2 bassoon: 2 horn. Written in Salzburg in July 1775, the first of five wind divertimento. See also K240, K252, K253 and K270 (12).

K214   MARCH IN C MAJOR.   Scored for 2 oboe: 2 horn: 2 trumpet: strings. Written in Salzburg 20 August 1775 (4).

K215   MARCH IN D MAJOR.   Scored for 2 oboe: 2 horn: 2 trumpet: strings. Written in Salzburg in August 1775 (4).

K216   CONCERTO FOR VIOLIN IN G MAJOR, *The Strasburg Concerto.* Scored for solo violin: 2 oboe: 2 horn: strings. Written in Salzburg 12 September 1775, known as the *Strasburg Concerto* on account of the theme in the last movement from a popular Strasburg dance tune (28).

Extract letter 216, L.M. to A.M., Salzburg, 6 October 1777:

"... *on Saturday I was at the play as there was a French epilogue. Brunetti had to play a concerto while the actors were changing dresses, and he played your lovely* Strasburg Concerto *most excellently.*"

Extract letter 228b, A.M. to L.M., Augsburg, 23 October 1777:

"... in the evening at supper I played my Strasburg Concerto *which went like oil. Everyone praised my beautiful pure tone."*

K217   ARIA FOR SOPRANO, *Vio Avete Un Cor Fedele.*   Scored for solo S: 2 oboe: 2 horn: strings. Written in Salzburg 26 October 1775 for Bacdassare Galuppi (1706–1785) (7).

K218   VIOLIN CONCERTO IN D MAJOR.   Scored for solo violin: 2 oboe: 2 horn: strings. Written in Salzburg in October 1775 again for concertmaster Brunetti (25).

K219   VIOLIN CONCERTO IN A MAJOR.   Scored for solo violin: 2 oboe: 2 horn: strings. Written in Salzburg 20 December 1775, the adagio of K261 in E flat written a year later to replace the original adagio considered by Brunetti as "too studied and too difficult" (30).

Extract letter 218, L.M. to A.M., Salzburg, 9 October 1777:

"I am still finding one or two little things which you need ... there is a whole music score for the wind instruments and the score of the adagio [K261] *you wrote especially for Brunetti, because he found the other one* [K219] *too artificial."*

K220   SHORT MASS IN C MAJOR.   Scored for solo S: A: T: B: choir: 2 trumpet/3 trombone: timpani: 2 violin: bass: organ. Written in 1775 in Salzburg, Colloredo commissioned the insertion of trumpets that were popular at the time, although the trumpet (and the flute) were not liked by A.M. This mass is known as the *Sparrow Mass* because of the chattering violin accompaniment in the Credo (18).

K221   KYRIE IN C MAJOR.

K222   OFFERTORY IN D MINO, *Misericordias Domini.*   Scored for choir: 2 violin/viola: bass: organ. Written in Munich in February 1775 and first performed to the Elector of Munich on 5 March 1775 in the Munich Court Chapel (7).

Extract letter 205, A.M. to Padre Martini, Salzburg, 4 September 1776:

"The regard, the esteem and the respect which I cherish for you illustrious person has prompted me to trouble you with this letter and to send you a

humble specimen of my music, which I submit to your masterly judgement
... a few days before my departure the Elector of Munich expressed a
desire to hear some of my contrapuntal compositions. I was therefore
obliged to write this motet [K222] *in a great hurry, in order to have*
the time to have the score copied, and thus enable it to be performed
during the offertory at High Mass on the following Sunday ... what
do you think of it?"

Padre Martini wrote back to A.M. on 18 December 1776:

"I received the motet [K222]. It was with great pleasure that I studied it ...
and I can tell you in all sincerity that I was singularly pleased with it,
finding it all that is required in modern music; good harmony, mature
modulation, a moderate pace in the violins, a natural connection of parts
and good taste. I am delighted with it, and since I had the pleasure of
hearing you at Bologna in the harpsichord, you have made great strides
with composition which must be persuaded even more by precise, for
music is of such a nature as to call for great exercise and study as long as
one lives."

Padre Martini requested a portrait of A.M., which was sent to him in
December 1777 by a local Salzburg painter; the portrait is now in the Martini
Conservatory in Bologna.

K223   HOSANNA IN C MAJOR.

K224   CHURCH SONATA IN F MAJOR.   Scored for 2 violin: bass: organ.
Written in Salzburg in early 1780 (3).

K225   CHURCH SONATA IN A MAJOR.   Scored for 2 violin: bass: organ.
Written in early 1780 in Salzburg (3).

K226   CANON, *O Sister's Bride.*

K227   CANON, *O Wondrous Beauty.*

K228   DOUBLE CANON IN F MAJOR.   Written for Franz Von Jacquin under
the manuscript of K228, "don't ever forget your true and faithful friend".

Von Jacquin was a supporter of A.M. and A.M. wrote a number of
complimentary compositions for him, which were performed and published

under Jacquin's name. K228 is one of them; there were four altogether, no trace of the other three remains.

K229   CANON IN C MAJOR, *She is Hence.*   Written in Vienna in 1782 (3).

K230   CANON IN C MINOR, *Selig, selig.*   Written in Vienna in 1782 (2).

K231   CANON IN B FLAT, *Lech mich im asch* (lick me on the arse).   Written in Vienna in 1772 but suppressed. It has been suggested that A.M. had Tourette syndrome (Gilles de la Tourette's Syndrome.) This is a hereditary condition, its symptoms being itching, tics, twitching, shaking, high pitched laugh, self-gratification, hyper-active, scatological references and a lavatorial vocabulary. All these symptoms A.M. had in abundance, which was relieved by playing the piano. Examples are to be found in his letters, particularly those to his cousin Maria Anna Thekla Mozart (known as Basle). She was the daughter of L.M.'s brother Franz Alois and lived in Ausburg. A.M. stayed with her from 1 October to 26 October 1777 and it seems likely that they had a sexual relationship.

Extract letter 236, A.M. to cousin, Mannheim, 5 November 1777:
> *"I shit on your nose and it will run down your chin. Have you got that spuni cunni business? Do tell me! Do you still love me? I am sure you do … wel … well that is alright, long live those who [word deleted]. I wish you good night but first shit in your bed and make it burst. Sleep soundly my love. Into your mouth your arse you'll shove … I'm off to fool about with myself then I'll sleep a bit. O my arse is burning like fire; what on earth does it mean perhaps some muck wants to come out."*

Extract letter 354, A.M. to cousin, 10 May 1779:
> *"Blow into my behind it's splendid food may it do you good."*

Extract letter 355, A.M. to cousin, 24 April 1780
> *"Well my dearest most beloved, most beautiful most charming and most amiable cousin hurry up and write to me, I need you."*

Extract letter 565, A.M. to wife, Berlin, 23 May 1789:
> *"I intend to sleep on 4th [June] with my darling little wife. Arrange your dear sweet nest very daintily for my little fellow deserves it indeed as he has really behaved himself very well and is only longing to possess your sweetish [word blotted out] just picture to yourself that rascal; as I write he crawls onto the table and looks up at me questionably. I however box his ears*

*fiercely and can hardly be restrained ... well now adieu ... I kiss you a
million times and am ever your most faithful husband W.A.M."*

K232   CANON for four voices.   Written for a Franz Freistadtler, known as
Gaulimauci, later became a well known opera singer (1).

K233   CANON IN B FLAT, *Lechmir.*   Written in Vienna in 1782. Possibly by
Trnka (2).

K234   CANON IN G MAJOR, *Bei der hitz.*   Possibly by Trnka (1).

K235   CANON FOR PIANO.

K236   ANDANTINO FOR PIANO IN E FLAT.   From Gluck's *Alceste.*

K237   MARCH IN D MAJOR.   Scored for 2 oboe: 2 bassoon: 2 trumpet:
2 violin: bass. Written in Salzburg August 1774 to be added to the serenade in
D major K203, *The Colloredo Serenade* (4).

K238   PIANO CONCERTO NO 6 IN B FLAT.   Scored for solo piano:
2 oboe/flute: 2 horn: strings. Written in Salzburg in January 1776.   *Age 20*

It is not certain why or for whom this was written, but A.M. certainly played
it on 4 October 1777 at a private concert of the Innkeeper Franz Albert. It
lasted from 3.30 to 8pm with liberal drink intervals. He also played K246
and K271.

called Serenade No 6 by NPR/Minneapolis

K239   SERENADE FOR TWO ORCHESTRAS IN D MAJOR in three
movements.   Scored for 2 violin: viola: double bass (solo): strings: <u>timpani</u>.
The strings and timpani as a separate orchestra, opposite to each other, set
against the solo instruments (12).   *Salzburg 1776*   *A a favorite of mine 6/06*

K240   DIVERTIMENTO FOR WIND IN B FLAT.   Scored for 2 oboe:
2 bassoon: 2 horn. Written in Salzburg January 1776 as "table music" to be
played at meal times for the Salzburg court (15).

K241   CHURCH SONATA IN G MAJOR.   Scored for 2 violin: bass: organ.
Written in Salzburg in 1776 (2).

K242   PIANO CONCERTO NO 7 FOR THREE PIANOS (or two pianos)
IN F MAJOR.   Scored for 3 solo pianos: 2 oboe: 2 horn: strings. Written in
Salzburg in February 1776 for Countess Antonia Lodrum and her two musical
daughters, Aloisia and Josepha, A.M.'s piano pupils. One of the daughters was
a poor pianist, therefore one of the parts is so slight that it can be left out,
hence the arrangement for two pianos (23).

Extract letter 227, L.M. to wife, Salzburg, 23 October 1777 (A.M. was with his
mother):

> *"So you are going to play the clavier concerto for three harpsichords.*
> *Perhaps Herr Stein's little daughter is going to play? Perhaps she will play*
> *on the first harpsichord, you on the second and father Stein on the third?*
> *This is only guesswork on my part! ... I am glad the Herr Stein's pianofortes*
> *are so good, but indeed they are expensive."*

The Stein family were celebrated keyboard manufacturers, building
harpsichords, organs and early pianofortes. L.M. purchased an early
instrument in 1763 as a practice piano for his son. Not until Beethoven did the
piano become regularly used. The best pianos still today are Steinways (see
K279–K284). Became Steinway's of New York in 1855.

K243   LITANY IN E FLAT, *Venerabili Altaris Sacramento.*   Scored for S: A:
T: B: choir: 2 oboe/flute: 2 bassoon: 2 horn: 3 trombone: strings: organ.
Written in Salzburg in March 1776 (34).

K244   CHURCH SONATA IN F MAJOR.   Scored for 2 violin: bass: organ.
Written in Salzburg in April 1776 (6).

K245   CHURCH SONATA IN D MAJOR.   Scored for 2 violin: bass: organ.
Written in Salzburg in April 1776 (3).

K246   PIANO CONCERTO NO 8 IN C MAJOR.   Scored for solo piano:
2 oboe: 2 horn: strings. Written in April 1776 for Countess Antonia von
Lutzow. This is known as the *Lutzow Concerto* and was extensively used as a
teaching piece by A.M. (23).

Extract letter 273, A.M. to L.M., Mannheim, 17 January 1778:

> *"I should mention that before dinner he* [Joseph Vogler, the music teacher at
> the Mannheim court] *had scrambled through my concerto at sight* [K246].
> *He took the first movement prestissimo, the Andante adagio and the rondo*

believe it or not prestissimo. He generally played the bass differently from the way I had written it, inventing now and then quite another harmony and even melody … well what good is it? That kind of sight reading and shitting are all one to me."

K247 DIVERTIMENTO IN F MAJOR. Scored for 2 horn: solo string (either violin, viola or cello). Written in Salzburg in June 1776 for Countess Antonio Lodrum, the wife of the Salzburg Marshall, and first performed on 13 June 1776. The two divertimento K247 and K287 are known as the *Lodrum Serenades* (33).

The wife of the Salzburg Marshall organised musical evenings and their house was the centre of Salzburg's musical life and therefore at this time very important to A.M. The second *Lodrum Serenade* was performed on the 16 June 1777 in the neighbouring garden of the Barisanis, who lived in the garden wing of the Palais Lodrum.

A member of the audience on 16 June later wrote:

"… supper as early as six – today. Then went to the Barisanis to hear music which young Mozart had written during the Octave [the week after a feast-day] for Countess Lodrum. It was quite magical and beautiful. This boy is amazing."

K248 MARCH IN F MAJOR. Scored for 2 horn: solo string. Written in Salzburg in June 1776 and generally played before K247, as an introduction (3).

K249 MARCH IN D MAJOR, *The Haffner March*. Scored for 2 oboe: 2 bassoon: 2 horn: 2 trumpet: strings. Written in Salzburg 20 July 1776 and played with the Haffner Serenade K250 (4).

K250 THE HAFFNER SERENADE IN D MAJOR in nine movements. Scored for 2 oboe/flute: 2 bassoon: 2 horn: 2 trumpet: solo violin: strings. Written in Salzburg in June 1776 commissioned by Siegmund Haffner for his sister Elizabeth and first performed on 21 July 1776 in his garden, on the eve of his sister's wedding to F.X. Spath. Lasting just over the hour, A.M.'s longest instrumental work. The commission stated *"light music to last about an hour"* (see K385) (68).

K251 DIVERTIMENTO IN D MAJOR in six movements. Scored for oboe: 2 horn: string quartet. Written in Salzburg in July 1776 to celebrate his sister's

(N.M.) "name day" (birthday) on 26 July aged 25. This was written to last for exactly 25 minutes (25).

K252   DIVERTIMENTO FOR WIND IN E FLAT.   Scored for 2 oboe: 2 bassoon: 2 horn. Written in Salzburg in January 1776 (12).

K253   DIVERTIMENTO FOR WIND IN F MAJOR.   Scored for 2 oboe: 2 bassoon: 2 horn. Written in Salzburg 1776 (16).

K254   DIVERTIMENTO IN B FLAT.   Scored for piano trio. Written in Salzburg in August 1776 (19).

K255   RECITATIVE AND ARIA FOR ALTO, *Ombra Ferlice*.   Scored for solo A: 2 oboe: 2 horn: strings. Written in Salzburg in September 1776 for the Castrato Francesco Fortina who was then performing an opera with an Italian touring company in Salzburg (7).

Extract letter 496, A.M. to L.M., Vienna, 12 April 1783:

> *"The next time you send me a parcel, please let the rondo for an alto voice which I composed for the Castrato who was with the Italian company in Salzburg take the same trip. When the weather gets warmer please make a search in the attic under the roof and send me some of your own church music. You have no reason whatever to be ashamed of it."*

L.M. by now, in 1783, was scared of composing any music as he realised that it was very second-rate compared to his son's. A.M. had criticised the father for the construction of some of his compositions.

K256   ARIA FOR TENOR, *Clarice Cara.*   Scored for 2 oboe: 2 horn: strings. Written in Salzburg 1776 (2).

K257   MASS IN C MAJOR, *The Credo Mass.*   Scored for solo S: A: T: B: choir: 2 oboe: 2 trumpet: 3 trombone: timpani: 2 violin: bass: organ. Written in Salzburg in September/November 1776. Known as the *Credo Mass* because every time the word *Credo* appears it is sung in unison and remains distinct from the general musical texture of the rest of the movement (29).

Extract letter 205, A.M. to Padre Martini, Salzburg, 4 September 1776:

> *"Meanwhile I am amusing myself by writing chamber music and music for*

the church [K257 and K259] *in which branches of composition we have two other excellent masters of counterpoint, Signore Haydn* [Michael, the younger brother of Joseph, who was organist at Salzburg Cathedral] *and Adlgasser. I thought you might like to see this."*

K258 MASS IN C MAJOR, *The Spaur Mass.* Scored for solo S: A: T: B: choir: 2 trumpet: timpani: 2 violin: bass: organ. Written in Salzburg in December 1776 for the consecration of Count von Spaur as Dean of the Cathedral in Salzburg (17).

Extract letter 306, L.M. to A.M. and wife, Salzburg, 28 May 1778:
    "At our practices Brunetti was always chattering about who would compose the consecration mass and was hoping for Haydn to get the commission from the Archbishop but the latter never replied ... I therefore produced Wolfgang's mass with the organ solo [K259] *taking the Kyrie from the Spaur mass.* [K258] *I had then copied out and received 6 ducats for my pains."*

K259 SHORT MASS IN C MAJOR, *The Organ Solo Mass.* Scored for solo S: A: T: B: choir: 2 trumpets: timpani: 2 violin: bass: organ. Known as the *Organ Solo Mass* due to the solo in the *Benedictus.* Written in Salzburg in December 1776 (16).

K260 OFFERTORY IN D MAJOR, *Venite Populi.* Scored for 2 S: 2 A: 2 T: 2 B: 2 violin: additional libretto: bass: organ. Written in Salzburg in mid-1776 and used in mass on Ascension Day in June 1776 (5).

K261 ADAGIO IN E FLAT, for the violin concerto in A Major K219. Scored for solo violin: flute: 2 horn: strings. Written in Salzburg in 1776 to replace the adagio in K219 (8).

K262 MASS IN C MAJOR, *The Long Mass.* Scored for solo S: A: T: B: choir: 2 oboe: 2 horn: 2 trumpet (or three trombone and timpani). Written in Salzburg in 1775 for the recently built St Peter's Church; known as the *Long Mass* because of its striking length, and performed on Easter Sunday, 7 April 1776, in Salzburg Cathedral (40).

K263 CHURCH SONATA IN C MAJOR. Scored for 2 trumpet: 2 violin: bass: organ. Written in Salzburg in December 1776 (3).

K264   VARIATIONS FOR PIANO IN C MAJOR, *Lison Dormait.*   Written in Paris in the late summer of 1778 (12).

Johann Hummel (1778–1837), a pupil of A.M.'s when aged 9, played these variations when on a three year long concert tour. He had a similar childhood to A.M. and was considered the next Mozart.

A critic wrote on 20 May 1789:
> "... a young pianoforte player aged 9, a native of Vienna and Mozart's pupil was heard in public here to the admiration of every listener, with Mozart's variations on *Lison Dormait* ... and this exceeds all expectations in agility, sureness and delicacy, but after all he was taught by Mozart."

K265   VARIATIONS FOR PIANO IN C MAJOR, *Ah, vous dirai'je maman?* (shall I tell you mummy?).   Written in Vienna in 1781/2. Twelve short variations from French songs (9).

From the publishers Torricella's prospectus when publishing this work in Vienna in 1875:
> "... newest fantasy variations by Kapp. A.W. Mozart. The eagerness with which the works of this famous master are on all sides awaited (these works will win the attention on the connoisseur with their beautiful art and freshness and so gentle to move our hearts with their melodies), persuades me to make these very beautiful variations my own, and thereby to be once more to be of service to the most esteemed lovers of music; for I offer them as a work which will bring fresh honour to it's creator. These variations, finely engraved, may already be had for 36 kr at my music shop. I shall spare no effort to provide the public with engraved copies of all the remaining variations of this master."

K266   STRING TRIO IN B FLAT.   Scored for 2 violins: bass. Written in Salzburg early in 1777 for light music, see Haffner, K250.

K267   FOUR CONTREDANCES IN G MAJOR: E FLAT: A MAJOR: D MAJOR. Scored for 2 oboe/flute: bassoon: 2 horn: 2 violin: bass. Written in Salzburg early in 1777 (7).

K268   CONCERTO FOR VIOLIN IN E FLAT.   Arranged in 1780 in Munich by the Violinist Johann Eek. Although the arrangement is made by Eek it was sketched out by A.M. but not certain how much composed by him. This must be considered a dubious work.

K269   RONDO CONCERTANTE FOR VIOLIN AND ORCHESTRA IN B FLAT. Scored for solo violin: 2 oboe: 2 horn: strings. Written in Salzburg in 1776 to replace the rondo in K207 for the concert master Brunetti (6).

Extract letter 208, L.M. to A.M. and wife, Salzburg, 25 September 1777:
> *"I shall give them together with the music for Andretter* [he was the war councillor in Salzburg] *some contredances the adagio and rondo you composed for Brunetti and anything else I might find for you to the messenger."*

K270   DIVERTIMENTO FOR WIND IN B FLAT.   Scored for 2 oboe: 2 bassoon: 2 horn. Written in January 1777 (11).

K271   PIANO CONCERTO NO 9 IN E FLAT, *The Jeanne Homme*.   Scored for solo piano: strings. Written in Salzburg in January 1777 for the celebrated Parisian pianist Mademoiselle Jeanne Homme who was on a European tour passing through Salzburg (33).

K272   RECITATIVE AND ARIA FOR SOPRANO, *Ah Lo Previdi*. Accompaniment 2 oboe: 2 horn: strings. Written in Salzburg in August 1777 for the famous soprano Josepha Duschek; the text by Paisiello. The Duschek family from Prague were great supporters of A.M. and became very friendly with him whilst he stayed with them in Prague in the Betranko Villa, now a museum (see also K527) (14).

K273   GRADUAL IN F MAJOR, *Sancta Maria*.   Scored for choir: strings: organ. Written in Salzburg 9 September 1777 shortly before leaving for Mannheim and Paris and intended as a prayer to the Virgin Mary, the feast of the Virgin Mary being on 12 September (4).

K274   CHURCH SONATA IN G MAJOR.   Scored for 2 violin: bass: organ. Written in Salzburg in 1777 (3).

K275   MASS IN B FLAT.   Scored for solo S: A: T: B: choir: 2 violin: bass: organ. Written in late 1777 and first performed in St Peter's Church in Salzburg on 21 December 1777 (20).

Extract letter 265, L.M. to A.M. and wife, Salzburg, 21/22 December 1777:
> *"I wrote the above yesterday, Sunday 21st December, on my return home, after the Hours service, when your Mass in B Flat was performed in which the castrato Francesco Ceccarelli sang it most excellently."*

K276 REGINA COELI IN C MAJOR.   Scored for solo: A: T: B: choir: 2 oboe: 2 trumpet: 2 violin: bass: timpani: organ. Written in Salzburg in 1779 as the third setting of the Regina Coeli in K108 and K127 (7).

K277 OFFERTORY IN F MAJOR, *Alma dei Creatoris*.   Scored for solo S: A: T: B: choir: 2 violin: bass: organ. Written in Salzburg in 1777 (5).

K278 CHURCH SONATA IN C MAJOR.   Scored for 2 oboe: 2 trumpet: 2 violin: timpani: bass: organ. Written in Salzburg in March/April 1777 (4).

K279 PIANO SONATA IN C MAJOR (14).

K280 PIANO SONATA IN F MAJOR (14).

K281 PIANO SONATA IN B FLAT (14).

K282 PIANO SONATA IN E FLAT (12).

K283 PIANO SONATA IN G MAJOR (14).

K284 PIANO SONATA IN D MAJOR (24).

These six first piano sonatas were written in Munich/Mannheim in early 1775; all of three movements. K281 under Haydn's influence, K284 commissioned by Baron Thaddaus von Durnitz (1756–1807). Durnitz was a major in the Austrian army and became A.M.'s patron for a short while. He also commissioned K292 and provided A.M. with support, but was very irregular in payments.

A.M. wrote 19 piano sonatas, see also K309, K310, K311, K330, K331, K332, K333, K457, K475 (a fantasia, not a true sonata), K533, K545, K570 and K576. There are also 17 sets of variations, some as short as 10 bars, and circa 65 other piano pieces. He wrote four sonatas aged 12 but these are lost. These six first sonatas were specifically written for the pianoforte not the harpsichord; they were written as a series intended for publication. A.M. used them frequently at concerts to show his virtuosity as a pianist.

Extract letter 225, A.M. to L.M., Augsburg, 17 October 1777:
> *"This time I shall begin at once with Stein's pianofortes. Before I had seen any of his make, Spath's claviers had always been my favourites. But now*

I much prefer Stein's, for they damp ever so much better than the Regensburg instruments. When I strike hard, I can keep my finger on the note or raise it, but the sound ceases the moment I have produced it. In whatever way I touch the keys, the tone is always even. It never jars, it is never stronger or weaker or entirely absent; in a word it is always even. It is true that he does not sell a pianoforte of this kind for less than 300 gulden, but the trouble and the labour which Stein puts in cannot be paid for. His instruments have this special advantage over others that they are made with escape action. Only one maker in a hundred bothers with this. But without an escapement it is impossible to avoid jangling and vibration after the note is struck. When you touch the keys, the hammers fall back again the moment after they have struck the strings whether you hold down the keys or release them. He himself told me that when he had finished making one of these claviers he sits down to it and tries all kinds of passages, runs and jumps, and he shaves and works away until it can do anything."

Later on the same letter:

"… here and at Munich I have played all my six sonatas by heart several times. I played the fifth in G [K283] at the great concert in the Stube. The last one in D sounds exquisite on Stein's pianoforte."

Extract letter 283a, A.M. to L.M., Mannheim, 7 February 1778:

"I will gladly give lessons as a favour, particularly when I see that my pupil has talent, inclination and anxiety to learn; but to be obliged to go to a house at a certain hour – or to have to wait at home for a pupil – is what I cannot do, no matter how much money it might bring in. I find it impossible so must leave it to those who do nothing but play the clavier. I am a composer and was born to be a Kapellmeister. I neither can nor ought to bury the talent for composition with which God in his goodness has so richly endowed me (I may say this without conceit, for I feel it now more than ever); and this I should be doing were I to take many pupils for it is a most unsettling metier. I would rather if I may speak plainly, neglect the clavier than composition for in my case the clavier with me is only a side-line though, thank God, a very good one."

age 22

From Torricella's prospectus:

"… from the pen of the famous and remarkable Herr Kappl. Mozart will be published by subscription by the under mentioned firm, three new clavier sonatas [K284, K333, K457] played at the theatre with general applause by Herr Mozart, and thus needs no further recommendation." (See also K242.)

K285   QUARTET FOR FLUTE AND STRINGS IN D MAJOR.   Scored for flute: violin: viola: cello. Written in Mannheim on 25 December 1777 for the amateur flautist Ferdinand de Jean, who was a doctor in the East India Company. A.M. disliked the flute and therefore by association he did not get on with de Jean (see K314) (17).

Extract letter 263a, A.M. to L.M., Mannheim, 18 December 1777:
> *"I shall soon have finished one quartet* [K285] *for the dreadful Indian Dutchman, that true friend of humanity."*

K286   NOCTURNO FOR FOUR ORCHESTRAS IN D MAJOR.   Scored for in four separate groups to be arranged around a large room, each group Scored for 2 horn: strings; one group being answered by the other in a triple echo (he was copying Vivaldi who first wrote for this effect). Written in Salzburg in the winter of 1776 for the New Year's Party at the Mirabelle Garden. This was a famous pleasure garden near Salzburg (16).

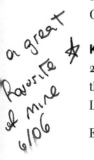

K287   DIVERTIMENTO IN B FLAT in six movements.   Scored for 2 horn: solo violin: strings. Written in Salzburg in June 1777 and known as the *Lodrum Divertimento*, the second *Lodrum* serenade. Written for Countess Lodrum (see K247) (46).   age 21

Extract letter 214, A.M. to L.M., Munich, 2 October 1777:
> *"… at Count Salerns during three days I played several things out of my head, and then the two Sassations I wrote for the Countess … you cannot imagine, how delighted the Count was but he really understands music he kept shouting 'Bravo' where other noblemen would take a pinch of snuff, !* blow their noses, clear their throats or start a conversation even. But he has *no idea what I can do. Why do these gentlemen believe what anyone tells them and never try to find it out for themselves? Yes, it is always the same, I am willing to submit to any test. I undertake to compete with any composer I have no fear."* √

Extract letter 217, A.M. to L.M., Munich, 6 October, 1777:
> *"As a finale I played my last cassation in B flat. They all opened their eyes. I played as though I were the finest fiddler in all Europe."*

K288   DIVERTIMENTO IN F MAJOR.   Fragment.

K289   DIVERTIMENTO IN E FLAT.   Scored for 2 oboe: 2 bassoon: 2 horn. Written in Salzburg in 1777 but spurious possibly not written by A.M.

K290   MARCH IN D MAJOR.   Scored for 2 horn: strings. Written in the summer of 1773 in Vienna for a garden party at Doctor Mesmer's house. Played at the same time as K205 (4).

K291   FUGUE.   An arrangement from Michael Haydn, written as an exercise for pupils.

K292   SONATA FOR BASSOON AND CELLO IN B FLAT.   Written in Munich in early 1775 for von Durnizt (see K284). A.M. was not paid (16).

K293   CONCERTO FOR OBOE IN F MAJOR.   Survives in 61 bars only. Commissioned by the oboist Franz Czerwenka in 1783.

K294   RECITATIVE AND ARIA FOR SOPRANO, *Alcandro, lo confesso.* Scored for solo S: 2 flute: 2 clarinet: 2 bassoon : 2 horn: strings. Written in Mannheim 28 February 1778, and in a second version in Vienna 19 March 1787 (K512). This work from a Metastasio text for A.M.'s sister-in-law Aloysia Webber (9).

Extract letter 292, A.M. to L.M., Mannheim, 28 February 1778:

> *"...for practice I have set to music the aria which has been so beautifully by Bach. Just because I know Bach's setting so well and like it so much, and because it is always ringing in my ears, I wish to see whether in spite of all this I could not write an aria totally unlike his ... so I returned it and made up my mind to compose it exactly for Mlle. Webber's voice. She has sung it exactly as I wished; this is now the best aria she has; and it will ensure her success wherever she goes."*

A.M. had asked Aloysia to marry him, she turned him down. He married her younger sister Constance in 1781.

K295   RECITATIVE AND ARIA FOR TENOR, 'Se al Labbo mio'.   Scored for solo T: 2 flute: 2 oboe: 2 bassoon: 2 horn: strings. Written in Mannheim 17 February 1778 for the tenor Raaffe (9).

Extract letter 292, A.M. to L.M., Mannheim, 28 February 1778:

> *"I was at Raaffe's yesterday and brought him an aria which I composed for him the other day ... He liked it enormously. One must treat a man like Raaffe in a particular way ... I asked him to tell me candidly if he did not like it, or if it did not suit his voice adding that I could alter it if he wished,*

or even quickly compose another. 'God forbid!' he said 'The aria must remain just as it is for nothing could be finer. But please shorten it a little for I am no longer able to sustain my notes.' 'Most gladly', I replied 'as much as you like for it is always easy to cut down, but not so easy to lengthen.'"

K296   SONATA FOR PIANO AND VIOLIN IN C MAJOR.   Written in Mannheim 11 March 1778 for Therese Serrarius, the daughter of his landlord in Mannheim (16).

Extract letter 217b, A.M. to L.M and N.M., Munich, 6 October 1777:
    "I send to my sister herewith six duets for clavicembalo [the Italian for harpsichord] and violin by Schoster which I have often played here. They are not bad! If I stay on here I shall write six in the same style as they are very popular here."

A.M. carried out this intention in Mannheim but writing only four in Mannheim (K296, K301, K303 and K305) and then two in Paris (K304 and K306).

K297   SYMPHONY NO 31 IN D MAJOR, *The Paris Symphony.*   Scored for 2 flute: 2 oboe: 2 clarinet: 2 bassoon: 2 horn: 2 trumpet: timpani: strings. Written in Paris in June 1778 (hence its name) and first performed on 12 June in Paris at the home of Count Sickingen, and then again on 18 June at the Concert Spirituel, the Corpus Christi Day concert (17).

From a critic in Paris, 26 June 1778:
    "... the Concert Spirituel on Corpus Christi Day began with a symphony by M. Mozart. This artist who from the tenderest age made a name for himself among harpsichord players, may today be ranked amongst the most able of composers."

Critic 15 July 1778, Paris:
    "This concert began with a symphony for full orchestra composed by Amadeo Mozards. We remarked of the great character of the first two movements, great richness of ideas, and as regards the third movement in which all the science of counterpoint shines forth the author attained the suffrages of the lovers of this kind of music that may interest the mind, but without ever touching the heart."

A.M. and his mother had arrived in Paris in April 1778, specifically to find a patron.

[handwritten margin note: Said to be the 1st symph. written by Mozart using the full complement of orchestral instruments]

Extract letter 309a, A.M. to L.M., Paris, 12 June 1778:

> *"I took some of my own compositions, as the Count had asked me to do. I brought along the new symphony which I have just finished and with which the Concert Spirituel will open at Corpus Christi. They both liked it very much and I too am pleased with it. But I cannot say whether it will be popular – and to tell the truth, I care very little, for who will not like it?"*

His mother's health had been failing and she died on 3 July. ✔

Extract letter 311, A.M. to L.M., Paris, 3 July 1778:

> *"Monsieur mon tres cher pere, I have very sad and distressing news to give you, my dear mother is very ill* [she died at 10.21pm on 3 July]. *She had been bled as in the past, and it was very necessary too. She felt quite well afterwards, but a few days later she complained of shivering and feverishness, accompanied by diarrhoea and headache ... as she got worse and worse, she could hardly speak and had lost her hearing, Baron Grimm sent us his doctor. They give me hope – but I have not much."*

This letter continues:

> *"I have had to compose a symphony of the Concert Spirituel. It was performed on Corpus Chiristi day with great applause and I hear, too, that there was a notice about it in the newspapers* [see above]. *So it has given great satisfaction."*

Extract letter 313, A.M. to L.M., Paris, 9 July 1778:

> *"I hope that you are now prepared to hear with fortitude one of the saddest and most painful stories; indeed my last letter of the 3rd that no good news could be hoped for. On that very same day, the third, at twenty-one minutes past ten at night, my mother fell asleep peacefully in the Lord; indeed when I wrote to you, she was already enjoying the blessings of heaven – for all was then over. I wrote to you during that night and I hope that you and my dear sister will forgive me for this slight but very necessary deception; for as I judged from my own grief and sorrow what yours would be, I could not indeed bring myself suddenly to shock you with this dreadful news ... Well His Heavenly and most holy will has been fulfilled. Let us therefore say a devout paternoster for her soul and turn our thoughts to other matters, for all things have there appropriate time. I am writing this in the house of Madam Epinay and Baron Grimm with whom I am now living* (she was Grimm's mistress). *I have a very pretty little room with a very pleasant view and, so far as my condition permits, I am happy."*

Extract letter from Baron Grimm to L.M., 27 July 1778:

"He is 'zu treuherzig' [too trusting], too inactive, too easy to catch , too little intent on the means that may lead to fortune. To make an impression here one has to be artful, enterprising, daring. To make his fortune I wish he had but half his talent and twice as much shrewdness and then I should not worry about him. For the rest, he can try but two ways here to make a living. The first is to give harpsichord lessons; but not to mention that one cannot get pupils without a great deal of activity and even Mountebankery, I am not sure that his health would be good enough for him to sustain that profession, for it is very tiring to run to the four corners of Paris and to exhaust oneself in explanations. And then his profession would not please him because it will keep him from writing, which is what he likes above all things."

Baron Grimm was a diplomat and a man of letters who had supported the family whilst on their Paris tour of 1764/5. He attempted to find full time employment for A.M. in Paris without success. They fell out and A.M. left him on 23 September en route back to Salzburg. A.M. later wrote:

"*Baron Grimm may be able to help children but not grown up people. Do not imagine that he is the same as he was.*"

K298   QUARTET FOR FLUTE, VIOLIN, VIOLA AND CELLO IN A MAJOR. Written probably in Vienna in 1786/7 as a musical joke, a parody against foreign musicians, particularly against Guiseppe Cambine, who was at that time a very popular violinist and composer whom A.M. thought useless (12).

K299   CONCERTO FOR FLUTE AND HARP IN C MAJOR.   Scored for solo flute: harp: 2 oboe: 2 horn: strings. Written in Paris in April 1778, commissioned by the Duke of Gines who played the flute and for his daughter, who played the harp (26).

Extract letter 305, A.M. to L.M., Paris, 14 May 1778:

"*I think I told you in my last letter the Duke of Gines whose daughter is my pupil in composition plays the flute extremely well and that she plays the harp magnificently.*"

Extract letter 319, A.M. to L.M., 31 July 1778:

"*For he has already had for the last four months , a concerto of mine for flute and harp for which he has not paid … what annoys me most of all here is that these stupid Frenchmen seem to think I am still seven years because that was my age when they first saw me.*"

K300   GAVOTTE FOR ORCHESTRA IN B FLAT.   Scored for 2 oboe: 2 bassoon: 2 horn: strings. First performed early in 1778 in Paris as a ballet accompaniment *Les Petits Reins* (24).

K301   SONATA FOR PIANO AND VIOLIN IN G MAJOR (13).

K302   SONATA FOR PIANO AND VIOLIN IN E FLAT (12).

K303   SONATA FOR PIANO AND VIOLIN IN C MAJOR (10).

K304   SONATA FOR PIANO AND VIOLIN IN E MINOR (18).

K305   SONATA FOR PIANO AND VIOLIN IN A MAJOR (11).

K306   SONATA FOR PIANO AND VIOLIN IN D MAJOR (21).

These six sonatas were dedicated to Electress Maria Elizabeth, the consort of Karl Theodor of Bavaria. They were written in Mannheim and Paris in 1778.

Extract letter 286a, A.M. to L.M., Mannheim, 14 February 1778:
> *"I can only compose at night, so that I cannot get up early as well; besides one is not always in the mood for working ... moreover you know that I become quite powerless whenever I am obliged to write for an instrument which I cannot bear* [See K285 Quartet for flute and strings], *hence as a diversion I compose something else such as the duets for clavier and violin which I love doing."*

K307   ARIETTE FOR SOPRANO IN C MAJOR, *Oiseauz Si Tous Les Ans* (Birds of every year).   An ariette is simpler and shorter type of aria no more than 20 bars. Written in Mannheim in the winter of 1777/8, the words by A. Farrand for Augusta Wendling (Gustel), the daughter of the flautist Johann Wendling (1).

Extract letter 283a, A.M. to L.M., Mannheim, 7 February 1778:
> *"... shortly after my arrival here I composed a French song for Mad. Gustel who gave me the words, and she sings it incomparably well. I have the honour to enclose it to you. At Wendilings it is sung every day for they are positively crazy about it."*

K308   ARIETTE FOR SOPRANO IN A FLAT, *Dans Un Bois Solitaire* (In The Lonely Garden). Written in Mannheim in the winter of 1777/8 again for Gustel, words by de la Motte (2).

Extract letter 292, A.M. to L.M., Mannheim, 28 February 1778:
> *"I have also promised the daughter some more ariettas and began one today. When they are ready I shall send them to you on 'small paper' as I did my first aria to her."*

K309   SONATA FOR PIANO IN C MAJOR.   Written in Mannheim in October/ November 1777 for Cannabich's young daughter Rosa, aged 14 years; she became a virtuiso pianist. (Cannabich was the leader of the Mannheim Orchestra considered then to be the best in Europe.) (17).

Extract letter 235, A.M. to L.M., 4 November 1777, Mannheim:
> *"He has* [Cannabich] *taken a good fancy to me. He has a young daughter* [Rosa] *who plays the clavier quite nicely, and in order to make a real friend of him, I am now working on a sonata for her which is almost finished, save the rondo. When I had composed the opening Allegro and the Andante I took them to their house and played both of them. Papa cannot imagine the applause which this sonata won."*

Extract letter 238a, A.M. to L.M., Mannheim, 8 November 1777:
> *"I wrote out at Cannabich's this morning the rondo to the sonata for his daughter, with the result that they refused to let me go."*

K310   SONATA FOR PIANO IN A MINOR.   Written in the summer of 1778 whilst his mother was ill. It is a very complex and difficult piece to play (22).

K311   SONATA FOR PIANO IN D MAJOR.   Started in Munich and finished in December 1777 in Mannheim, for one of the Freysinger sisters, Maria Anna, an amateur piano player (15).

Extract letter 254, A.M. to Cousin Maria Anna Mozart ("The Basle"), Mannheim, 3rd December 1777:
> *"As for the sonata she must possess herself in patience for a little longer. If it had been for my dear Coz, it would have been finished long ago. Who knows that she hasn't forgotten all about it ... I send you a great dollop of kisses, slap, bang and wallop."*

[handwritten margin note: Anne Mclean has mentioned this and wld have played it for us if there had been more time 5/06]

K312   SONATA FOR PIANO IN G MINOR.   Unfinished; only the first movement, written, in the summer 1790.

K313   CONCERTO FOR FLUTE IN G MAJOR.   Scored for solo flute: 2 oboe: 2 horn: strings (26).

K314   CONCERTO FOR FLUTE IN D MAJOR or FOR OBOE IN C MAJOR. Both this and K313 written in early 1778 in Mannheim, for the amateur flautist Dr Ferdinand de Jean (18).

Extract letter 278 in the form of a poem, A.M. to his mother, Worms, 31 January 1778:

> *O, Mother mine!*
> *Butter is fine*
> *Praise and thanks be to Him*
> *We're alive and full of vim*
> *Through the world we dash*
> *Though we're rather short of cash*
> *But we won't find this provoking*
> *And none of us are choking …*
> *The Concerto for Paris I'll keep tis more fitting*
> *I'll scribble it there one day when I'm shitting* [See K313 and 314]
> *To embrace you and kiss your hands so fair*
> *But first in my pants I'll shit I swear*
> *Your faithful child with distemper wild Trazom* [palindrome]

Extract letter 286a, A.M. to L.M., Mannheim, 14 February 1778:

> *"… by the time however I hope to have made enough money for Mama's journey home … M. de Jean is also leaving for Paris tomorrow and because I have only finished two concertos* [K313 and314] *and three quartets* [K285] *he has sent 96 gulden, that is four gulden too little. Evidently supposing that this was half of the two hundred, but he must pay me in full, for that is our agreement."* [He did not pay in full.]

K315   ANDANTE FOR FLUTE AND ORCHESTRA IN C MAJOR.   Scored for solo flute: 2 oboe: 2 horn: strings. Written in Salzburg late 1779/80. This andante is intended as a far simpler slow movement for either K313 or K314 as de Jean found the originals too difficult to play. Fredrich Ramm, however, played the original andante for K314 on the oboe on 13 February 1778 at a private musical party at the Cannabich's house, where A.M. conducted.

K316   RECITATIVE AND ARIA FOR SOPRANO, *Popoli di Tessaglia.*   Scored for Solo S: oboe: bassoon: 2 horn: strings. Written in July/August 1778 for Aloysia Weber, sister of Constance, and presented to her in Mannheim on 8 January 1779, words by Calzabigi, from Gluck's *Alceste* (11).

Extract letter 318, A.M. to Aloysia, Paris, 30 July 1778:

"*... and I shall send in the same parcel the Popoli di Tessaglia, which is already half finished. If you are pleased with it as I am, I shall be delighted. Meanwhile until I have the pleasure of hearing from you whether you really like this scena, for since I have composed it for you alone – I desire no other praise than yours. I can only say that of all my compositions of this kind, this scena is the best I have ever composed.*"

K317   MASS IN C MAJOR, *The Coronation Mass.*   Scored for solo S; A: T: B: choir: 2 oboe: 2 horn: 2 trumpet: 3 trombone: timpani: 2 violin: bass: organ. Written in Salzburg 23 March 1779 and known as the *Coronation Mass*, as it is traditionally believed to have been written for the ceremonial crowning of a miraculous image of the Virgin Mary in the church of Maria-Plain in the mountains above Salzburg. This ceremony was carried out each year on the fifth Sunday after Pentecost.

However later research shows that it acquired the name *Coronation Mass* when Antonio Salieri conducted its performance at the coronation of Leopold II in Prague in early 1791 (27).

This mass and K337 are the last of the Salzburg Masses. Tension between A.M. and the Archbishop Colloredo came to a head. The Archbishop requested constant restrictions of the form and length of masses. This culminated in 1781 by A.M. resigning, and "*being kicked down the stairs*"; a new life was opening up for him in Vienna. A.M. lived permanently in Vienna from the summer of 1781.

Antonio Salieri (1750–1825) was made court composer and Italian opera conductor in Vienna. It is certain that Salieri was jealous of A.M's superior gifts, but an admission that he supposedly made in his final illness that he poisoned A.M. is now discredited. (Peter Schaffer's play/film *Amadeus* brings this point out).

K318   SYMPHONY NO 32 IN G MAJOR in one movement. Used as the overture to Zaide (K344).   Scored for 2 flute: 2 oboe: 2 bassoon: 4 horn: 2 trumpet: timpani: strings. Written in Salzburg 26 April 1779 and used by the theatrical productions of J.H. Bohm, a travelling theatre group with Salzburg as their headquarters (8).

K319 SYMPHONY NO 33 IN B FLAT.   Scored for 2 oboe: 2 bassoon: 2 horn: strings. Written in Salzburg 9 July 1779, with an additional minuet written in Vienna 1785 making a full four movement symphony (23).

Published by Artaria in May 1787 and performed in a benefit concert in Frankfurt on 15 October 1790, cost of entry 2 florins for boxes and stalls and 24 Kr for the gallery. The second concert planned for the 17 October was cancelled due to poor ticket sales.

K320 SERENADE IN D MAJOR, *The Posthorn Serenade* in seven movements.   Scored for 2 flute/piccolo: 2 oboe: 2 bassoon: 2 horn: posthorn: 2 trumpet: timpani: strings. Written in Salzburg 3 August 1779, the use of the posthorn in the second minuet giving the name to the work. First performed on 24 September 1779 in the Kolleglenplatz for the Salzburg University Final music the end of the academic year (45).

K321 VESPERS DE DOMINICA IN C MAJOR.   Scored for solo S: A: T: B: choir: 2 trumpet (or bassoon/trombone): 2 violin: bass: organ. Written in Salzburg in 1779. Why and for whom is not known, not performed in A.M's lifetime (30).

K322 KYRIE IN E FLAT, fragment.

K323 KYRIE IN C MAJOR.   Mostly lost; only the lyrics and fragments remain.

K324 HYMN, *Salus Informorium.*

K325 SANCTA MARIA, spurious.

K326 HYMN, *Justem Deduxit Dominus.*

K327 HYMN, *Adoramus.*

These four hymns under Gasparini's influence.

K328 CHURCH SONATA IN C MAJOR.   Scored for 2 violin: bass: organ. Written in Salzburg early in 1779 as part of the Coronation Mass (K317) (8).

This was written separately from the *Coronation Mass*, as together the time factor of 45 minutes was too long for the Archbishop.

K329   CHURCH SONATA IN C MAJOR.

K330   SONATA FOR PIANO IN C MAJOR (18).

K331   SONATA FOR PIANO IN A MAJOR, *Alla Turka*. For the Elector of Munich (24).

K332   SONATA FOR PIANO IN F MAJOR (19).

This is the second group of piano sonatas written in Munich and Paris in 1781 and K332 written in Vienna in 1783. A.M. used them extensively in performances; when in Vienna between 1781 and 1784 he gave a large number of piano performances.

K333   SONATA FOR PIANO IN B FLAT.   Written in Linz in 1774 as a one-off exercise (21).

K334   DIVERTIMENTO IN D MAJOR in 6 movements.   Scored for 2 horn: solo violin: strings. Written in Salzburg in the summer of 1780 for the Robinig family, a wealthy mine-owning family in Salzburg.

Extract letter 414, A.M. to L.M., Vienna, 4 July 1781:
> *"I badly need the three cassations – those in F and B flat* [K247 and K287] *would do me for the time being … but you might also have the one in D copied* [K334] *for me some time and sent on later, for the charge for copying is very heavy in Vienna; in addition to which they copy most atrociously."*

Towards the end of 1779 a report in a music journal in Augsburg noted:
> "… 'but some excellent good genius' have tried their fortune abroad the mention of a couple of whom must not be admitted. One such is Leopold Mozart … his instruction for the violin which was printed here has made his name famous [this was financed by the Robinig family]. His son Herr Chevalier Wolfgang has over the years become celebrated for his exceptional power on the clavier … he displayed the whole of his powers at a magnificent public concert [in Augsburg]."

K335   TWO MARCHES IN D MAJOR.   Scored for 2 oboe/flute: 2 horn: 2 trumpet: strings. Written in Salzburg in August 1779. One of the marches was played with K320 on 24 September 1779 for the Salzburg University "Finale Music" concert (8).

K336 CHURCH SONATA IN C MAJOR.   Scored for 2 violin: bass: organ. Written in Salzburg in March 1780. This is the last of the 17 church sonatas. This one specifically intended to be played between the Epistle and the Gospel of the Mass (5).

K337 MASS IN C MAJOR, *The Solemn Mass*   Scored for solo S: A: T: B: choir: 2 oboe: 2 bassoon: 2 trumpet (or 3 trombone): timpani: 2 violin: bass: organ. Written in Salzburg in March 1780, the last of the *Salzburg Masses* (K317) (22).

K338 SYMPHONY NO 34 IN C MAJOR in three movements.   Scored for 2 oboe: 2 bassoon: 2 horn: 2 trumpet: timpani: strings. Written in Salzburg 29 August 1780, the last of the *Salzburg Symphonies*, and first performed in the Salzburg Court concert in early September 1780. The minuet after the first movement was excluded but later to appear in K409 (21).

Extract letter 398, A.M. to L.M., Vienna, 11 April 1781:
> *"You asked me whether I had been to see Bono* [court composer in Vienna], *why, it was at his house that we went through my symphony for the second time … I forgot to tell you the other day that at the concert my symphony in C major went magnifique and had the greatest success. There were forty violins, the wind instruments were all doubled, there were ten violas, ten double bases, eight violinceollo, six bassoons."*

Played for the benefit of the newly established Society of Musicians at a Grand Musical Concert on 3 April 1781. This society was formed in 1771 and reconstituted in 1781 on the lines of the London Musical Society to help families of musicians.

An announcement for this concert:
> "… a concert by Mozart … He was already here himself as a boy aged seven, and even then earned the general applause of the public, partly then in the manner of composition and partly in that of art altogether."

A.M. had the Viennese orchestras to compose for, in a much grander style than the Salzburg court orchestra.

K339 SOLEMN VESPERS IN C MAJOR.   Scored for solo S: A: T: B: choir (bassoon): 2 trumpet/3 trombone: timpani: 2 violin: bass: organ. Written in Salzburg in 1780 for a specific saint's day, unknown (27).

K340   KYRIE.   This is not traced, probably dubious.

K341   KYRIE IN D MAJOR.   Scored for S: A: T: B: 2 flute: 2 oboe: 2 clarinet: 2 bassoon: 4 horn: 2 trumpet: timpani: strings: organ. Written in Munich between January and March 1781 to show the Elector of Munich A.M.'s capability of church musical composition, specifically requested and part of his request for employment , which was unsuccessful (see also K331) (6).

K342   OFFERTORY, *Benedicite Angeli.*

K343   TWO SACRED SONGS IN F MAJOR AND C MAJOR, *O Gotts Lamm, Aus Aegypten.*   Scored for solo S and B. Written in Prague or in Vienna in 1782, under the influence of German Protestantism. This was specifically commissioned (2).

K344   ZAIDE, *Das Serail.*   A singspiel in two acts, unfinished, with no overture (see K318) or final chorus. Scored for S: 2–3 T: 2 B: 2 flute: 2 oboe: 2 bassoon: 2 horn: 2 trumpet: timpani: strings. Written in Salzburg in the winter of 1779/80, the libretto arranged by J.A. Schachter (court trumpeter in Salzburg) and first performed early in 1781 possibly either by Schikaneder or Bohm, the concert Singspiel Group. Joseph II had recently given authority for a new National Singspiel. A.M.'s second "Turkish Opera", see K384. The Turkish theme was greatly in vogue in 1780/81 (88).

Extract letter 390, A.M. to L.M., Salzburg, 18 January 1781:
> *"Do not forget to bring my little watch with you, I hope we shall be able to go over to Augsburg where we can have the enamel repaired. I should like you to bring Schachtner's operetta too [K344]. There are some people who come to the Cannabach's who might just as well hear a thing of this kind."*

K345   CHORUS AND MUSIC to *Thamos, King of Egypt.*   Scored for solo B: chorus: 2 flute: 2 oboe: 2 bassoon: 2 horn: 2 trumpet: 2 trombone: timpani: strings. Libretto by Baron Gebler, started in Vienna in 1773 and completed in Salzburg in 1779; first performed by the touring group Bohm in Salzburg in the winter of 1779 (45).

Extract letter 187, L.M. to wife, Vienna 18 September 1773:
> *"Wolfgang is composing something most enthusiastically."*

Extract letter 481, A.M. to L.M., Vienna 15 February 1783:
> *"I am extremely sorry that I shall not be able to use the music to* Thamos,

but this piece, which failed to please here, is now among the neglected works which are no longer performed. For the sake of the music alone it might possibly be given again but this seems unlikely."

It was used again in a play by Plumicke, called *Lanassa*.

Baron Gebler to a friend in Vienna, 31 May 1773:
> "… should my *Thamos* have the honour of being performed here, I could oblige with the music for the choruses which had been not at all badly set, and were thoroughly revised here by the Chevalier [possibly by Gluch not A.M.]."

K346   VOCAL ENSEMBLE FOR THREE VOICES, *Luci care, Luci belle* Scored for 2 S: B: with 3 basset horn accompaniment.   Written in Vienna between 1783 and 1786 (see K436–K439) (2).

K347   CANON IN D MAJOR, *Lasst uns ziehn.* (Let us go).   Written in Vienna in 1782 (1).

K348   CANON IN G MAJOR, *V'amo di core Teneramente* (1).

K349   SONG IN G MAJOR, *Was frag ich Viel* (How many I ask).   There are two versions of this song, piano or mandolin accompaniment, words by J. Miller (3).

K350   SONG, *Sleep my little prince.* (Spurious.)

K351   SONG IN C MAJOR, *Komm liebe Zither* (Come dear Zither). Written in Munich in the winter of 1780/1781 with mandolin accompaniment (2).

K352   VARIATION FOR PIANO IN F MAJOR.   Eight piano variations of the march Gretry's *Les Maraiges Samnites.* The theme suggested by Archbishop Colloredo. Written in Vienna in June 1781 (see also K359 and K360).

Extract letter 410, A.M. to L.M., Vienna 13 June 1781:
> *"At each concert I played twice and the last time when the concert was over I went on playing the variations (for which the Archbishop gave me the theme) for a whole hour and with such general applause that if the Archbishop had any vestige of humanity, he must have felt delighted. But, instead of showing me – or not showing me for all I care – his pleasure and*

satisfaction he treats me like a street urchin and tells me to my face to clear out, adding that he can get hundreds to serve him better that I ... The archbishop on two occasions said the most insulting things to me and I never said a word in reply ... Well, if he does not want me that is exactly what I wish ... Count Arco hurls me out of the room and gives me a kick on my behind."

This is the end of his employment with Collorado and from now on A.M. goes alone. All his major masterpieces are composed from mid-summer 1781 to his death in 1791.

K353   VARIATIONS FOR PIANO IN E FLAT, *La Belle Francoise.*   Written in Paris in 1781 from a popular French song "whistled at the time by all" (9).

K354   VARIATIONS FOR PIANO IN E FLAT, in twelve variations from the theme *Je suis Lindor.*   Written in Paris early in 1778 from a song in Beaumarchais's *The Barber of Seville,* the original music written by Baudron (18).

K355   MINUET FOR PIANO IN D MAJOR.   Written in Vienna in 1786 (3).

K356   ADAJIO FOR GLASS-HARMONICA IN C MAJOR.   Written in Vienna in 1791 for the blind glass-harmonica virtuoso Marianne Kirchgassner, and together with K617 she took these two adajios on her European tour and had great success with them, particularly in London. Kirchgassner (1769–1808) became blind as a child and was the only virtuoso player on the "armonica".

A critic from the *Morning Post,* London, 17 March 1794, when Marianne Kirchgassner played K356 and K617:
> "Her taste is chastened, and the dulcet notes of her instrument would be delightful indeed, were they more powerful and articulate; but we believe the most perfect execution cannot make them. In a smaller room, and an audience less numerous, the effect must be enchanting. Though the accompaniments were kept very much under, they were occasionally too loud."

K357   PIANO SONATA FOR FOUR HANDS IN G MAJOR.   Only the allegro, 98 bars, and the andante, 158 bars, survive.

K358   PIANO SONATA FOR FOUR HANDS IN B FLAT.   Written in Salzburg late 1773/early 1774 for his sister N.M. and himself to play on one keyboard. It was also used for his pupils (20).

K359   VARIATIONS FOR PIANO AND VIOLIN IN G MAJOR.   Written in Vienna in the summer 1781 from a popular French song *La Bergere Cevimene* (15).

K360   VARIATIONS FOR PIANO AND VIOLIN IN G MINOR in six variations. Written in Vienna in June 1781 from a popular French song *J'ai perdu mon Amant*. Both K359/360 were written for a pupil, Countess Thiennes de Rumbeke (7).

Extract letter 414, A.M. to L.M., Vienna, 20 June 1781:

> *"Unless I have something particularly important to tell you I shall write to you once a week, as I am very busy just now. I must close this letter as I have some variations for my beautiful Countess, my pupil, to finish off. Adieu, I kiss your hands a thousand times and embrace my sister with all my heart and am ever yours."*

K361   SERENADE FOR WINDS IN B FLAT, *The Gran Partita* in seven movements.   Scored for 2 oboe: 2 clarinet: 2 basset horn: 2 bassoon: 4 horn: bass (alternative). Written in Munich in 1781, laid aside and then completed in Vienna early in 1784, the first performance on 23 March 1784 in a benefit concert for Anton Stadler, the clarinettist, in the Burgtheatre in Vienna (54).

Quote from the music critic Schink on 24 March 1784:

> "I heard music for wind instruments today Herr Mozart ... at each instrument sat a master. Oh, what an effect it made, glorious and grand, excellent and sublime. His music is fantastic."

[handwritten margin note: Listen for this... one of his greatest orchestral works. "M. at his best in handling wind instruments."]

K362   MARCH TO IDOMINEO (see K366).   It is not known why this march was added to the opera.

K363   THREE DANCE MINUETS IN D MAJOR, B FLAT AND D MAJOR. Scored for 2 oboe: 2 bassoon: 2 horn: 2 trumpet: timpani: 2 violin: bass. Written in Vienna in late 1782/3 (3).

K364   SINFONIA CONCERTANTE FOR VIOLIN AND VIOLA IN E FLAT. Scored for solo violin: solo viola: 2 oboe: 2 horn: strings. Written in Salzburg

[handwritten margin note: Age 23!]

in the autumn of 1779; intended to be played in Mannheim and Paris as this form of setting was very popular at the time (33).

K365   PIANO CONCERTO NO 10 IN E FLAT FOR TWO PIANOS.   Scored for 2 solo pianos: 2 oboe: 2 bassoon: 2 horn: strings. Written in Salzburg in 1779; A.M. and N.M. played this together on 3 September 1780 (24).   *age 23*

On 23 November 1781 A.M. played K365 at Auernhammer's house with his host's daughter Josepha. She was very musically gifted but was ugly; she fell in love with her teacher only to be rejected by him. They also played K365 on the morning of 26 May 1782. This was a subscription concert held in the morning in the refreshment pavilion of a public park opened by Joseph II in 1775.

K366   IDOMENEO.   Opera Seria. Scored for 3 S: 3 T: B: chorus: 2 flute: 2 oboe: 2 clarinet: 2 bassoon: 2 horn: 2 trumpet: timpani: strings. The Italian libretto written by Abbate Giambasttista Varesco, court Chaplin in Salzburg (see also K422). Written in Salzburg in the winter of 1780/81. Commissioned for the Munich carnival and first performed in the Munich Hoftheatre on 29 January 1781. The fee was 200 gulden (186).

Extract letter 356, A.M. to L.M., Munich, 8 November 1780:

"With regard to the libretto, the Count [Seeau] *says that Abbate Veresco need not copy it out again before sending it ... but I think that he ought to finish writing the text ... some slight alterations will have to be made here and there, to suit exactly what I require."*

Extract letter 362, A.M. to L.M., Munich, 22 November 1780:

"You must however forgive me if I do not send you much in return, for every minute is precious, and as it is, I can generally only compose in the evenings, as the mornings here are so dark, then I have to dress ... when the castrato comes, I have to sing with him, for I have to teach him his whole part, as if he were a child."

Extract letter 383, A.M. to L.M., Munich, 30 December 1780:

"A happy new year! Forgive me for not writing much this time, but I am up to my eyes in work. I have not quite finished the third act, and as there is no extra ballet, but only an appropriate divertissement in the opera, I have the honour of composing the music for that as well." [See K367 ballet music for *Idomeneo.*]

Extract letter 389, A.M. to L.M., Munich, 3 January 1781:

"My head and my hands are so full of act III that it would be no wonder if I were to turn onto the third act myself, this fact alone has cost me more trouble than the whole of the opera, for there is hardly a scene in it which is not extremely interesting."

Extract letter 387, A.M. to L.M., Munich, 10 and 11 January 1781:

"The latest news is that the opera has yet again been postponed for a week. The dress rehearsal will not now take place until the 27th – my birthday, mark you this – and the first performance on the 29th... but I am delighted as it will give us an opportunity of further and more careful rehearsals."

Extract letter 390, A.M. to L.M., Munich, 18 January 1781:

"But I can only send you my most important news. The rehearsal of act three went off splendidly. It was considered much superior to the first two acts."

Between 8 November 1780 and 18 January 1781 A.M. wrote 16 letters to his father, the longest being 8 pages; L.M. returned 20.

From a Munich newspaper, 1 February 1781:

"On the 29th day of last month the first performance of the opera *Idomeneo* took place at the new opera house here. The text, music and translation – all are by natives of Salzburg ... attracted everyone's admiration."

K367   BALLET MUSIC FOR IDOMENEO.   See extract of letter 383 above (15).

K368   RECITATIVE AND ARIA FOR SOPRANO, *Ma che vi Fece.* Accompaniment 2 flute: 2 bassoon: 2 horn: strings. Written in Salzburg in 1779/80, words by Metastasio, possibly for the soprano Elizabeth Wendling. The words of this song:*"When I seek to avoid one perilous rock, I throw myself upon another far worse than the first."* (9).

K369   SCENE AND ARIA FOR SOPRANO, *Misera! Deve Son.* Accompaniment 2 flute: 2 horn: strings. Written in Munich 8 March 1781 for the Countess Baumgartner (7).

Extract letter 358, A.M. to L.M., Munich, 13 November 1780:

"Cannabich and I lunched yesterday with Countess Baumgarten, nee Lerchenfeld. My friend is positively worshipped by her family and now I am too. It is the best and most useful house for me here, for owing to their

kindness all has gone well with me and, God willing, will continue to do so. It is she who has a Fox's tail sliding out of her Arse and, oh Vanity an Odd looking watch-chain hanging Under her eaR and a fine ring. I have seen It myself Through death should take me, unfortunate fellow without a nasal Extremity."

The underlined initialled letters spell out the word "favourite" the Countess's position at the Elector of Munich's court. She was his mistress. A.M. was certain that his letters were being intercepted.

K370   QUARTET FOR STRING AND WIND IN F MAJOR.   Scored for oboe: violin: viola: cello. Written in Munich in January/February 1781 for the oboist Friedrich Ramm (17).

K371   RONDO FOR HORN AND ORCHESTRA IN E FLAT.   Scored for solo horn: 2 oboe: 2 horn: strings. Written in Vienna 21 March 1781 for the Salzburg horn player Ignaz Leitgeb. This work survives only in sketch form, 119 bars (5).

K372   SONATA FOR PIANO AND VIOLIN IN B FLAT.   Written in Vienna 24 March 1781, only the Allegro completed. Stadler finished the sonata (15).

K373   RONDO FOR VIOLIN AND ORCHESTRA IN C MAJOR.   Scored for solo violin: 2 oboe: 2 horn: strings. Written in Vienna 23 April 1781 for the Salzburg Court Orchestra leader, Antonio Brunetti (4).

Extract letter 397, A.M. to L.M., Vienna, 8 April 1781 (but dated 8 April 1780):
  "Today, for I am writing at eleven o'clock at night, we had a concert where three of my compositions, the new ones of course, a rondo for a concerto for Brunetti, a sonata with violin accompaniment for myself [K379] which I composed last night between eleven and twelve. But in order to be able to finish it, I only wrote out the accompaniment for Brunetti and retained my own part in my head perfectly."

K374   RECITATIVE AND ARIA FOR SOPRANO.   Scored for solo S: 2 oboe: 2 horn: strings. Written in Vienna in 1781 for the castrato Ceccarelli. First performed on 8 April 1781 for the Archbishop of Salzburg and his retinue in residence in Vienna during the celebrations for the Emperor Joseph II (9).

K375   SERENADE FOR WINDS IN E FLAT.   Scored for 2 oboe: 2 clarinet:

2 bassoon: 2 horn. Written in Vienna in October 1781, with a second version added in 1782 with 2 further oboes (28).

Extract letter 431, A.M. to L.M., Vienna, 3 November 1781:

> *"At twelve o'clock I drove out to Baroness Waldstadten at Leopold stadt, where I spent my name day* [31 October]. *At eleven o'clock at night I was treated to a serenade performed by two clarinets, two horns and two bassoons, and that too of my own composition* [K375] *... for I wrote it for St. Theresa's Day for Frau von Hickel's sister, or rather the sister-in-law of Herr von Hickel, the Court Painter at whose house it was performed for the first time. The six gentlemen who executed it are poor beggars who however, play quite well together particularly the first clarinet and the two horns ... I wrote it rather carefully, it has won great applause as on St Theresa's night it was played in three separate places."*

K376   SONATA FOR PIANO AND VIOLIN IN F MAJOR. Written in Vienna in the summer of 1781 (16).

From Cramner's music magazine, Hamburg, 4 April 1783:

> "Six sonatas for the piano with violin accompaniment by Wolfg. Amadie Mozdart published by Artaria in Vienna."

Publicity from the publisher:

> "These sonatas are unique in their kind. Rich in new ideas and traces of the author's great musical genius. Very brilliant, and completely suited to their instruments. At the same time the violin accompaniment is so ingeniously combined with the clavier part that both instruments are kept in equal prominence, so that the sonatas call for as skilled a violinist as a clavier player. However it is impossible to give a full description of these original works. Amateurs and connoisseurs should first play them through for themselves and they will then perceive that we have in no way exaggerated."

By now A.M., living in Vienna, married, with their first child born 17 June 1783, was attracting large audiences; to quote from Cramner again, 9 May 1783:

> "Vienna 23rd March 1783. Last night the famous Herr Chevalier Mozart held a musical concert in the National Theatre at which pieces of his highly admired compositions were played. The concert was honoured by an exceptionally large concourse and the two new concertos and other fantasias which Herr Mozart played on the fortepiano were received with

the loudest applause. Our Monarch, who against his habit, attended the whole of this concert, as well as the entire audience, accorded him [A.M.] such unanimous applause as has never been heard of here before. The receipts for the concert were estimated to have amounted to 1,600 gulden in all."

K377   SONATA FOR PIANO AND VIOLIN IN F MAJOR.   Written in Vienna in the summer of 1781 (19).

K378   SONATA FOR PIANO AND VIOLIN IN B FLAT.   Written in Salzburg early in 1779, or in Vienna in 1781 (19).

K379   SONATA FOR PIANO AND VIOLIN IN G MAJOR.   Written in Vienna in April 1781 (see also K373) (20).

K380   SONATA FOR PIANO AND VIOLIN IN E FLAT. Written in Vienna in the summer of 1781. These 5 sonatas K376–K380 and K296 were published by Artario and Co. in Vienna in November 1781 and dedicated to Elizabeth Auernhammer at three ducats each (19).

K381   PIANO SONATA FOR FOUR HANDS IN D MAJOR.   Written in Salzburg in mid-1773 (see K358) (18).

K382   RONDO FOR PIANO AND ORCHESTRA IN D MAJOR.   Scored for solo piano: flute: 2 oboe: 2 horn: 2 trumpet: timpani: strings. Written in Vienna in March 1782 as a new finale for the piano concerto K175, which was written in 1773 (8).

Extract letter 445, A.M. to L.M., Vienna, 23 March 1782:
   "I am sending you at the same time, the last rondo [K382] *which I composed for my concerto in D major* [K175] *and which is making such a furore in Vienna. But I beg you to guard it like a jewel and not to give it to a soul to play ... I composed it especially for myself to play – and no-one else but my dear sister must play it."*

Extract letter 483, A.M. to L.M., Vienna, 12 March 1783:
   "My sister-in-law, Madame Lange, gave her concert yesterday in the theatre and I played a concerto [K175 and K382]; *the theatre was very full and I was received again by the Viennese public so cordially that I really ought to feel delighted. I had already left the platform but the audience would not*

stop clapping and so I had to repeat the rondo upon which there was a torrent of applause."

The first performance of the rondo with K175 was first performed by A.M. on 3 March 1782 as the first "Lent Concerts" he gave in Vienna. Also he improvised a fantasy on the piano especially for the benefit of Clementi, his rival in piano playing. It is of note that Clementi shortly afterwards left Vienna. It was considered that he knew he could not win over A.M. There is alas no proof of this fantasy.

Cramner's report, Hamburg, 2 March 1783:
> "… this young genius (Beethoven) deserves support to enable him to travel he would be sure to become a second Wolfgang Amadeus Mozart if he progressed as he has begun *(aged 13)*."

This is the first printed report on Beethoven. He played to A.M. in Vienna in 1787, and may have had lessons from him, but was called back to Bonn as his mother had died. Beethoven's early works were greatly influenced by Mozart.

K383   ARIA FOR SOPRANO, *Nehmt meinen dank* (Receive my thanks). Scored for solo S: lute: oboe: bassoon: strings. Written in Vienna 10 April 1782 (4).

K384   DIE ENTFUHRUNG AUS DEM SERAIL (The Elopement from the harem), Singspiel opera. At first titled *Belmont Und Constance.*   Scored for 2 S: 2 T: B: chorus: 2 flute/piccolo: 2 oboe: 2 clarinet/basset horn: 2 bassoon: 2 horn: 2 trumpet: timpani: strings. Written in the autumn 1781 to spring 1782, after the play by C. F. Bretzner, libretto by Gottlieb Stephanie, who also commissioned the work, the fee being 100 ducats. First performed in Vienna at the Burgtheatre on 16 July 1782, A.M. conducting. Joseph II was present and remarked afterwards that the "Opera had very many notes"; A.M. replied "exactly the necessary number" (Niemetschek) (128).

A.M.'s report on the first performance lost, but see letter extract 453 below. The first two performances brought in 1,200 florins. It was repeated 41 times, making this opera his greatest stage success in his lifetime, as the theme on Turkish oriental settings was very much in vogue at the time. See also K344.

Extract letter 453, A.M. to L.M., Vienna, 20 July 1782:
> *"I hope you have received safely my last letter. Informing you of the good reception of my opera. It was given yesterday for the second time. Can you*

really believe it, but yesterday there was an even stronger cabal against it than on the first evening! The whole first act was accompanied by hissing. But indeed they could not prevent loud shouts of Bravo during the arias. I was relying on the closing trio, but as ill luck would have it Fisher [Bass Osonin] *went wrong, which made Dauer* [Tenor Pedrillo] *go wrong too and Adam Berger* [Tenor Belmonte] *alone could not sustain the trio."*

Various critics at the time:

"... the opera has been received with very notable applause in Vienna. Applause it owes not to itself but to the excellent music of Herr Mozart ... an undeniable product of musical genius ... his song uncommonly eloquent as the language of heat and of nature and that he shows altogether the right ideas of the true purpose of the most beautiful of all human arts."

But there were opponents; by Bretzner:

"A certain individual, Mozart by name, in Vienna has had the audacity to misuse my drama *Belmonte and Constance* for an opera text. I herewith protest most solemnly against this infringement of my rights and I reserve the right to take the matter further."

He also criticised Stephanie the librettist for altering the shape and style of his original play:

"Is that that what you called improvement?"

Bretzner eventually becomes an ally of A.M.'s and in 1794 writes:

"... this *(Cosi)* is charming and altogether admirable music of this master by the immortal Mozart."

Gluck heard the opera on 6 August 1782, the performance at his request, congratulated A.M. and invited him to dinner on 8 August. Gluck was at this time by far the most popular composer of operas.

A comment by Goethe in December 1785:

"... everyone declared himself for the music. The first time they played it tolerably, the second time it was badly played and I even went out. But the piece survived and everyone now praises the music.

K385　SYMPHONY NO 35 IN D MAJOR, *The Haffner* in four movements. Scored for 2 flute: 2 oboe: 2 clarinet: 2 bassoon: 2 horn: 2 trumpet: timpani: strings. Written in Vienna, July and early August 1782, originally as a serenade in five movements, the minuet now lost. Flutes and clarinets were added later in 1782 at L.M.'s request, to celebrate the raising of Sigmund [handwritten: Mayor of Salzburg] Haffner to the nobility, which took place on 29 July 1782. The first full performance took place on 23 March 1783 at a subscription concert, the [handwritten: age 27] entrance 25 florins, played to a full house (22). [handwritten: at Vienna's Royal Burgtheater w. Emperor Joseph II present. M. much]

Extract letter 453, A.M. to L.M., Vienna, 20 July 1782: [handwritten: age 26] [handwritten: gratified at Joseph's "delight" and applause]

> "... *and now you ask me to write a new symphony! How on earth can I do so? ... well I must just spend the night over it, for that is the only way I can finish it ... I shall work as fast as possible. And, as far as haste permits I shall of course turn out good work.*"

Extract letter 456, A.M. to L.M., Vienna, 31 July 1782:

> "... *you see my intentions are good – only what one cannot do, one cannot do! I am really unable to scribble off inferior stuff. So I cannot send you the whole symphony until the next post day.*"

A.M. married C.M. (Constance, nee Webber) on Sunday 4 August 1782. The wedding took place in the parish of St Stephen's Vienna. The marriage contract:

> "This day, between the well and nobly born Herr Wolfgang Mozart, [handwritten: age 26] Kapellmeister, Batchelor as bridegroom on the one part and the noble spinster Constantia Webber the legitimately begotten daughter of minor years [she was 17] of the noble Herr Webber."

K386 RONDO FOR PIANO AND ORCHESTRA IN A MAJOR. Scored for solo piano: 2 oboe: 2 horn: strings. Written in Vienna 19 October 1782 and intended as a finale for piano concerto K414 (7).

K387 QUARTET FOR STRINGS IN G MAJOR, *The Haydn Quartets.* The first of the six string quartets written for Joseph Haydn, the others being K421, K428, K458, K464 and K465. K387 was written in Vienna 31 December 1782. All six quartets were complete in 1785 and dedicated to Haydn on 1 September 1785, and published by Artaria and Co. in October 1785 (30).

Extract letter 529, A.M. to Joseph Haydn, Vienna, 1 September 1785:

> "*To my dear friend Haydn, a father who has decided to send his sons into the great world though it is his duty to entrust them to the protection and guidance of a man who was very celebrated at the time and who, moreover, happened to be his best friend. In like manner I send my six sons to you, most celebrated and very dear friend. They are indeed the fruit of a long and laborious study ... your good opinion encourages me to offer them to you*"

and leads me to hope that you will not consider them wholly unworthy of your favour."

On 15 January 1785 A.M. and friends played the first three quartets with Haydn present, and the second three quartets on 12 February 1785 with both Haydn and L.M. present. Haydn declared to L.M. that:

"Before God and as an honest man, I tell you that your son is the greatest composer known to me either in person or by name. He has taste, and what is more, the most profound knowledge of composition." (See extract letter 523: K428.)

A.M. had become friendly with Haydn at this time, as Haydn lived in Vienna in 1785. A.M. was greatly influenced by Haydn's opus 33 quartets, written in 1781. A.M. knew and played these works frequently.

K388   SERENADE FOR WINDS IN C MINOR.   Scored for 2 oboe: 2 clarinet: 2 bassoon: 2 horn. Written in Vienna in July 1782, and then transcribed into a string quintet in 1788, see K406. Possibly written for the two Stadler brothers, Anton and Johann, both fine clarinettists (26).

Extract letter 455, A.M. to L.M., Vienna, 27 July 1782:

"Mon tres cher Pere, it has been quite impossible to do more for you, for I have had to compose in a great hurry, a serenade [K388] *but only for wind instruments, otherwise I could have used it for you too."*

His father was a noted violinist and at his request the transcription into strings took place for him to play (see K406).

K389   DUET FOR TWO TENORS, *Welch Angstliches beden.*   Scored for 2 T: flute: oboe: bassoon: 2 horn: strings. Written in Vienna in April/May 1782 originally intended to be included in K384, see above, as Bretzner's wording was used.

K390   SONG, *An die Hoffmung.*   Piano accompaniment in D minor. Written in Vienna in 1781/2, words by J.T. Hermes (2).

K391   SONG, *An die Einsamkeit.* Piano accompaniment in B flat Written in Vienna in 1781/2, words by J.T. Hermes (3).

K392   SONG, *Verdankt sei es dem Glanz.* Piano accompaniment. Written in Vienna 1781/2, words by J.T. Hermes (4).

K393 SOLFEGGIO FOR SOPRANO. A solfeggio is a vocal exercise to "warm the voice". Written in August 1782 for C.M., now his wife.

K394 PRELUDE AND FUGUE FOR PIANO IN C MAJOR. Written in Vienna in early 1782 for his students (10).

Extract letter 447, A.M. to N.M., Vienna, 20 April 1782:

> *"I send you herewith a prelude and a three part fugue* [K394], *the reason why I did not reply to your letter at once was that on account of the wearisome labour of writing these small notes, I could not finish the composition any sooner. And even so, it is awkwardly done, for the prelude ought to come first and the fugue to follow, but I composed the fugue first and wrote it down quickly while I was also thinking out the prelude."*

K395 CAPRICCIO AND FUGUE FOR PIANO IN C MAJOR. Written in Munich in October 1777 (4).

K396 FANTASIA FOR PIANO IN C MINOR. Written in Vienna early in 1782 (13).

K397 FANTASIA FOR PIANO IN D MINOR. Written in Vienna early in 1782. These four fantasias influenced by the Bach family and used for piano exercises for his students in Vienna in 1782, where he had over 40 students at the height of his teaching career (7).

K398 VARIATIONS FOR PIANO IN F MAJOR, *Salve tu, Domine.* Written in Vienna in March 1783 (7).

K399 SUITE FOR PIANO IN C MAJOR. Written in early 1782 in Vienna, a Sarabande included later (11).

K400 SONATA FOR PIANO IN B FLAT. Written in Vienna in the summer of 1781 as a musical joke dedicated to Sophia and Constance Weber, his future sister-in-law and his wife. It ends with a loud discord in B flat. This sonata was added to by Stadler (12).

K401 FUGUE FOR PIANO IN G MINOR. Written in Vienna in the early spring of 1782, incomplete and again later completed by Stadler, who arranged it as a piano duet (5).

K402   SONATA FOR PIANO AND VIOLIN IN A MAJOR.   Written in Vienna in the summer of 1782 for C.M. again incomplete and finished by Stadler (11).

K403   SONATA FOR PIANO AND VIOLIN IN C MAJOR.   Written in Vienna in the summer of 1782, again completed by Stadler (14).

The two Stadler brothers were both excellent performers on the clarinet and the basset horn and were employed in the court orchestra in Vienna. Anton played K581 and K622.

K404   SONATA FOR PIANO AND VIOLIN IN C MAJOR.   Andante and allegro only. Written in Vienna in 1782 as a musical joke, poking fun at C.M. (3).

K405   STRING QUARTETS.   Arrangement of five fugues in C MINOR, E FLAT, E MAJOR, D MINOR, D MAJOR; after J.S. Bach. Scored for 2 violin: viola: cello. Written in Vienna in 1782, originally scored for keyboard. The fugues and preludes of J.S. Bach were from the well-tempered Clavier book 2 of the 48 numbered 2, 5, 7, 8 and 9. Commissioned by Baron Gottfreid von Swieten, an amateur music lover in the Austrian Diplomatic Service. An arrangement of a further nine preludes and fugues for string quartet are included in K405, but there appears to be some dispute over who arranged them.

K406   QUINTET FOR STRINGS IN C MINOR.   This quintet is a transcription of the Wind Serenade in C minor K388. Written in Vienna in April 1788 and offered on subscription together with K515 and K516 for four ducats from Michael Puchberg, a fellow mason of A.M.'s. (23).

Extract letter 553, A.M. to Puchberg, Vienna, June 1788:

> *"Dearest brother, your true friendship and brotherly love embolden me to ask a great favour of you. I still owe you eight ducats. Apart from the fact that at the moment I am not in a position to pay you back, my confidence in you is so boundless that I have to implore you to help me out with a hundred gulden until next week ... By that time I shall certainly have received my subscription money, and then shall be able quite easily to pay you back 136 gulden with my warmest thanks."* [A.M. received one hundred ducats.]

Johann Puchberg (1741–1822) lived in Vienna and was a fellow mason and friend of A.M.'s from 1787. He worked as a textile manager for the firm of

Salliet. Between 1787 and A.M.'s death in 1791 he lent him c.1500 florins. After his death on 5 December 1791 Puchberg made no claim for the repayment of this sum, although some of it had been repaid by A.M. in his lifetime. He also advanced further sums to C.M. after her husband's death which she later repaid in full. Puchberg died in 1822 in poverty. K542 and K563 as well as K406 were dedicated to him.

K407   QUINTET FOR HORN AND STRINGS IN E FLAT.   Scored for horn: violin: 2 viola: cello. Written in Vienna at the end of 1782 for the horn player Joseph Leutgeb (18).

Joseph Leutgeb (1732–1811) was friendly with A.M for all the composer's life. He was the horn player in the court orchestra at Salzburg. In 1777 he moved to Vienna and ran a cheesemonger's shop whilst continuing his musical career. A.M. also wrote K412, K417, K447 and K495 for Leutgeb.

K408   THREE MARCHES FOR ORCHESTRA:

March no. 1 in C major.   Scored for 2 oboe: 2 horn; trumpet: timpani: strings. Written in Vienna in 1782.

March no. 2 in D major: The Haffner.   Scored for 2 oboe: 2 bassoon: 2 horn: 2 trumpet: timpani: strings. Written in Vienna in the summer of 1782.

Extract letter 458, A.M. to L.M., Vienna, 7 August 1782:
> *"I send you herewith a short march. I only hope it will reach you in good time and be to your taste. The first allegro [K385, The Haffner Symphony] must be played with great fire; the last – as fast as possible."*

March no. 3 in C Major.   Scored for 2 flute: 2 bassoon: 2 horn: 2 trumpet: timpani: strings. Written in the summer 1782.

K409   MINUET TO SYMPHONY NO 34 [K338] IN C MAJOR.   Scored for 2 flute: 2 oboe: 2 bassoon: 2 horn: 2 trumpet: timpani: strings. Written in Vienna in May 1782 (5).

K410   ADAJIO FOR BASSOON/BASSET HORN IN F MAJOR.   Scored for 2 basset horn: bassoon. Written in Vienna in the winter of 1785, incomplete; only 27 bars exist. Experimental music written for Anton Stadler and two of his friends for the fun of combining woodwind instruments together (2).

K411   ADAJIO FOR CLARINET AND BASSET HORN IN B FLAT.   Scored for 2 clarinet: 3 basset horns. Written in Vienna in the winter of 1785, incomplete, 106 bars surviving. Intended as a solemn entrance procession of A.M.'s Masonic Lodge as the woodwind combination appropriate to Masonic ritual (7).

K412   CONCERTO FOR HORN IN D MAJOR.   Scored for solo horn: 2 oboe: 2 bassoon: strings. Written in Vienna in 1791, the last horn concerto, thought to have been written initially in 1782 together with K407 but now established by Tyson as from 1791 from the paper watermarks. Leutgeb again the recipient, and although his teeth were troublesome could still play the horn well enough. Great hilarity between A.M. and Leutgeb, see K495 (8).

K413   PIANO CONCERTO NO 11 IN F MAJOR.   Scored for solo piano: 2 oboe: 2 bassoon: 2 horn: strings. Written in Vienna in the summer/autumn of 1782 for the subscription concerts A.M. was planning early in 1783 (see below K414 and K415).

Extract letter 476, A.M. to L.M., Vienna, 28 December 1782:   *age 26*
> "The evening is therefore the only time I have for composing. And of that I can never be sure as I am often asked to perform at concerts. There are still two concerts wanting to make up the series of subscription concerts. These concertos are a happy medium between what is too easy and too difficult; they are very brilliant, pleasing to the ear and natural without being vapid. There are passages here and there from which the connoisseurs alone can derive satisfaction; but these passages are written in such a way that the less learned cannot fail to be pleased though without knowing why. I am distributing the tickets at six ducats a piece."

Extract letter 477, A.M. to L.M., Vienna, 4 January 1783:
> "Only three concertos are being published and the price is now four ducats."

Extract letter 479, A.M. to L.M., Vienna, 22 January 1783:
> "You need have no fear that the three concertos are too dear. I think after all I deserve at least a ducat for each concerto and besides, I should like to know who can get them copied for a ducat."

K414   PIANO NO 12 IN A MAJOR.   Scored for solo piano: 2 oboe: 2 horn: strings. Written in Vienna in mid-1782, actually the first of the three (27).

K415   PIANO CONCERTO NO 13 IN C MAJOR.   Scored for solo piano: 2 oboe: 2 bassoon: 2 horn: 2 trumpet: timpani: strings. Written in Vienna late 1782 (26).

Extract letter 487, A.M. to J.G. Sieber, a music publisher in Paris, Vienna, 26 April 1783:

"Well, this letter is to inform you that I have three piano concertos ready, which can be performed with a full orchestra, or with oboes and horns, or merely a quatro. Artaria wants to engrave them, but I give you, my friend, the first refusal. And in order to avoid delay I shall quote my lowest terms to you. If you give me thirty Louis D'or for them, the matter is settled." [Artaria actually published them in March 1785.]

From the newspaper *Vienna Zietung,* 15 January 1783:

"Herr Kapellmeister Mozart herewith apprises the highly honoured publication of his three new, recently finished piano concertos. The three concertos, which may be performed either with a large orchestra with wind instruments or merely a quatro, viz. with 2 violins, 1 viola, 1 cello will not appear until the beginning of April this year and will be issued, finally copied and supervised by himself, only to those who have subscribed thereto. The present serves to give the present news that the subscription tickets may be had of him for four ducats, counting from the 20th of this month to the end of March."

It was apparently not a successful subscription. A.M. offered them to a Paris publisher (see above). They were eventually published by Artaria (see above). A.M. felt they were too expensive at a ducat for each subscription. What price now?

Vienna Zietung, 27 September 1783:

"At Johann Traeg's in the Vinegar-market house, no 654, first floor, new manuscript music is again to be had, viz the three latest piano concerto by Mozart at 10 florins."

Vienna Zietung, 5 March 1785:

"At the art establishment of Artaria Comp. – are newly to be had three pianoforte concertos by Herr Kapellmeister Mozart in A Major, F Major and C have been engraved and each is to be have at 2fl.30kr.

The selling of music generally was offered by subscription first and then the public could purchase the music in manuscript form. Since there were no performance fees or copyright, income could only come from selling to the publishing firms or by public subscription concerts. A.M. played these three ✓✓ concertos in his lifetime at least 30 times. How often the other, later ones?

K416   RECITATIVE AND RONDO FOR SOPRANO, *Mia Speranza Adorata.*
Scored for solo S: 2 oboe: 2 bassoon: 2 horn: strings. Written in Vienna
8 January 1783 for his sister-in-law Aloysia Lange (nee Weber) (10).

Extract letter 478, A.M. to L.M., Vienna, 8 January 1783:
   *"I have to finish a rondo this evening for my sister-in-law, which she is to
   sing on Saturday at a big concert in the Mehlgrube."*

K417   CONCERTO FOR HORN NO 2 IN E FLAT.   Scored for solo horn:
2 oboe: 2 horn: strings. Written in Vienna 27 May 1783 for Joseph Leutgeb
(see K412) (14).

K418   ARIA FOR SOPRANO, *Vorrei Spiegarui* (Away with the Mischief).
Scored for solo S: 2 oboe: 2 bassoon: 2 horn: strings. Written in Vienna 20
June 1783, again for Aloysia Lange (see also K178) (7).

K419   ARIA FOR SOPRANO, *No, No, Che non sei Capace.*   Scored for solo S:
2 oboe: 2 horn: 2 trumpet: timpani: strings. Written in Vienna with K418 for
Aloysia Lange (4).

From *Anfossi's Opera Magazine*:
   "The two arias [K418, K419] have been set to music by Signor Maestro
   Mozzart to oblige Signora Lange, those written by Maestro Anfossi not
   being commensurate with her ability but meant for someone else ... this is
   herewith made known to all, in order that honour should be done to whom
   it should be due, without in any way doing harm to the fame of the already
   sufficiently well-known Neapolitan Anfossi."

Italian and German opera were in competition, the arias above, were written
in both languages; A.M's sister-in-law sang in Italian but A.M. preferred
German.

On 30 June 1783:
   "Madame Lange sang at the Italian opera, and the public showed, in the
   face of every intrigue between the two opera styles and Salieri how much it
   valued her great talent."

K420   ARIA FOR TENOR, *Perpieta non Ricercate.*   Scored for solo T:
2 clarinet: 2 bassoon: 2 horn: strings. Written in Vienna 21 June 1783 for
Johann Adamberger (6).

Extract letter 493, A.M. to L.M., Vienna, 21 June 1783:

> *"This will have to be a very short letter. For the new Italian opera is being produced in which for the first time two German singers are appearing. Madame Lange, my sister-in-law and Adamberger and I have to compose to arias for her and a rondo for him."*

Johann Adamberger (1740–1804), a member of the same Masonic lodge as A.M., sang many parts and helped A.M. to promote his works.

K421 QUARTET FOR STRINGS IN D MINOR. Written in Vienna in June 1783, the second Haydn Quartet (28).

Their first child Raimund was born on 17 June 1783, died 19 August 1783 "of intestinal cramp". In all they had 6 children; only 2 survived into adulthood.

K422 OPERA, *L'Oca del Cairo* (The Cairo Goose). Scored for 3 S: 2 T: 2 B: chorus: 2 oboe: 2 bassoon: 2 horn: strings. Written in Salzburg and in Vienna in 1783, the libretto by Abbate Giambattista Varesco, the court Chaplain in Salzburg. A.M. disliked both the Chaplin and the libretto (68).

Extract letter 500, A.M. to L.M., Vienna, 6 December 1783:

> *"I have only three more arias to compose and then the first act of my opera [K422] will be finished ... I should therefore be sorry to have written the music to no purpose, I mean if what is absolutely necessary doesn't take place, neither you or Abbate Varesco nor I have noticed that it will have a very bad effect and even cause the entire failure of the opera. If neither of the two principle female singers appear on stage until the very last moment the patience of the orchestra might hold out for one act but certainly not for a second act."*

K423 DUET FOR VIOLIN AND VIOLA IN G MAJOR. Written in Salzburg in the summer of 1783. The original commission of this and K424 was for Michael Haydn but through illness he was unable to carry out this commission and requested A.M. to do so (17). His salary had been stopped by Colloredo until he finished these two duets. A.M. completed them in Haydn's name.

K424 DUET FOR VIOLIN AND VIOLA IN G MAJOR. Written in Salzburg in the summer of 1783 (21).

Extract letter 500, A.M. to L.M., Vienna, 6 December 1783:

> *"Please send me as soon as possible my Idomeneo, the two violin duets [Haydn] and Bach's fugues [K405] ... further will you ask Tomaselli to let us*

have the prescription for the eczema ointment which has done us excellent services."

Michael Haydn (1737–1806) was the younger brother to Joseph (1732–1809). He became the concert master to the Archbishop of Salzburg in 1763 and then organist in 1781 when A.M. moved to Vienna. They remained good friends and these two duets resulted from this friendship. A.M. also composed K444, incorporated into a Michael Haydn symphony.

Michael was totally dominated by his brother Joseph and although he had considerable success, it was always under the shadow of Joseph.

K425   SYMPHONY NO 36 IN C MAJOR, *The Linz* in four movements. Scored for 2 oboe: 2 bassoon: 2 horn: 2 trumpet: timpani: strings. Written in Linz in October 1783 at "breakneck speed" for old Count Thun and first performed on 4 November 1783 in the theatre at Linz. A.M. conducted (38).

Extract letter 499, A.M. to L.M., Linz, 31 October 1783:
  "I really cannot tell you what kindness the family are showering on us [A.M. staying with the Thun family], on Tuesday November 4th I am giving a concert in the theatre here, and, as I have not a single symphony with me, I am writing a new one at breakneck speed which must be finished by that time. Well, I must close, because I really must get down to work."

Extract letter 504, A.M. to L.M., Vienna, 20 February 1784:
  "The symphony [K425] is in the original score which you might arrange to have copied sometime. You can then send it back to me or even give it away, or have it performed anywhere you like."

Extract letter 519, L.M. to N.M., Salzburg, 17 September 1784:
  "... on the following day we had a big concert at Barisani's [the court physician at Salzburg] where your brothers new and excellent symphony was performed under my direction."

The *Linz Symphony* was played again on 1 April 1784 in one of A.M.'s great musical concerts for his own benefit at the I & R National Court Theatre in Vienna. A.M. revised some of it as he felt it had been written in too much of a hurry.

K426   FUGUE FOR TWO PIANOS IN C MINOR.   Written in Vienna 29 December 1783 and later re-arranged as a string quartet (K546) in 1788 with a new introduction to the original fugue by J.S. Bach (4).

K427   MASS IN C MINOR.   Scored for solo 2 S: T: B: choir (specific directions as 8 in the choir, 2 of each voice): flute: 2 oboe: 2 bassoon: 2 horn: 2 trumpet: 3 trombone: timpani: strings: organ. Written in July 1782 and further worked on in August 1783 but remained unfinished. First performance of the Kyrie and Gloria on 26 October 1783 at St Peter's Church Salzburg, with C.M. performing one of the soprano parts. This mass is shrouded in mystery; it either celebrates the birth of their first child or indeed to celebrate their marriage a year earlier (63).

Extract letter 477, A.M. to L.M., Vienna, 4 January 1783:
> *"I made the promise in my heart of hearts and hope to be able to keep it. When I made it my wife was still single. The score of half the mass is still lying here waiting to be finished, and is the best proof that I really made the promise to finish."*

Part of this mass was later used in *Davidde Penitente* (K469). It was sung in early December 1787 at the Church of St Nicholas in Prague.

A report of this occasion:
> "On 6 December, at the Church of St Nicholas, a musical mass written by Herr Mozart, the composer so favoured here, was performed, and everyone admitted that in this kind of composition he is the complete master."

K428   QUARTET FOR STRINGS IN E FLAT.   Written in Vienna in June and July in 1783, the third of the Haydn quartets (28).

K429   CANTATA, *To The Soul Of The Universe.*   Scored for solo T: 2 T: B: flute: 2 oboe: clarinet: 2 horn: bassoon: strings. Written in Vienna in 1785, the words by I.L. Haskhka, uncompleted but finished by Stadler (8).

Mathias Stadler (1744–1827) a tenor and violin teacher to the choir in Salzburg.

K430   LO SPOSO DELUSO.   Comic opera; the husband deceived. Scored for 2 S: 2 T: 2 flute: 2 oboe: 2 bassoon: 2 horn: 2 trumpet: timpani: strings. Libretto, possibly by Da Ponte but this is not certain. The opera was not finished as A.M. considered the words unsatisfactory (19).

Extract letter 495, A.M. to L.M. Vienna, 5 July 1783:
> *"An Italian poet here has now brought me a libretto which I shall perhaps adopt, if he agrees to trim and adjust it in accordance with my wishes."*

Lorenzo Da Ponte (1749–1838): it is not certain he wrote the libretto but he later collaborated with A.M. in his three finest operas, *The Marriage of Figaro, Don Giovanni* and *Cosi Fan Tutte.* After A.M.'s death in 1791 he worked in various cities, London, New York and in Italy. His move from one city to another was usually marked by scandal or intrigue. He died in America in 1838.

K431   RECITATIVE AND ARIA FOR TENOR, *Misero O Sogno.*   Scored for solo T: 2 flute: 2 bassoon: 2 horn: strings. Written in Vienna in December 1783 for the tenor Johann Adamburger and first performed on 22 December 1783 at the Vienna Society of Musicians concert (11).

A.M. also played one of his piano concertos.

Extract letter 502 A.M. to L.M., Vienna, 24 December 1783:
> *"The day before yesterday, Monday, we had another grand concert of the Society, when I played a concerto and Adamburger sang a rondo of my composition* [K431]. *The concert was repeated yesterday, but a violinist played a concerto in my place. The day before yesterday the theatre was full. Yesterday it was empty. I should add that it was the violinist's first performance."*

K432   RECITATIVE AND ARIA FOR BASS, *Cosi dunque Tradisci.*   Scored for solo B: 2 flute: 2 oboe: 2 bassoon: 2 horn: strings. Written in Vienna in 1783 for the celebrated bass Johann Fischer (5).

Johann Fischer 1745–1825: A.M. became friendly with him in 1783.   Fischer sang in most of the European centres and also in the later of A.M.'s operas.

K433   ARIETTA FOR BASS, *Men are always seeking.*   Written in Vienna in 1783, to be included in a play by Goldoni, but this play possibly did not materialise (7).

K434   TRIO FOR TENOR AND BASS, *Il Regno deue Amozoni.*   Scored for T: 2 B: 2 oboe: 2 bassoon: 2 trumpet: strings. Written in Vienna at the end of 1783, 106 bars only, possibly therefore incomplete.

K435   ARIA FOR TENOR.   Scored for solo T: flute: oboe: 2 bassoon: 2 horn: 2 trumpet: timpani: strings. Written in Vienna in 1783, again for the playwrite Goldoni.

Extract letter 480, A.M. to L.M, Vienna, 5 February 1783:

> *"I do not believe that the Italian opera will keep going for long, and besides, I hold with the Germans. I prefer German opera, even though it means for more trouble for me … I am now writing a German opera for myself. I have chosen Goldoni's comedy* Il Servitore di due Padroni *… but we are keeping a secret until it is quite finished. Well what do you think of this scheme? Do you not think that I shall make a good thing of it?"*

Nothing further was heard of this project.

K436   VOCAL ENSEMBLE FOR THREE VOICES.   Scored for 2 S: B: 3 basset horn (2).

K437   VOCAL ENSEMBLE FOR THREE VOICES.   Scored for 2 S: B: 2 clarinet: basset horn: (4).

K438   VOCAL ENSEMBLE FOR THREE VOICES.   Scored for 2 S: B: 2 clarinet: basset horn (2).

K439   VOCAL ENSEMBLE FOR THREE VOICES.   Scored for 2 S: B: 3 basset horn. (1)

These four works K436–K439 were written in 1783 and 1786, libretto from Metastasio's "songs of good fellowship". A.M. was in 1783 giving singing lessons to Baron Gottfried von Jacquin and his sister and their circle of singing friends.

Gottfried von Jacquin (1727–1817) was a botanist and professor at the university of Vienna. A keen singer with his family and his three children, he was a pupil of A.M. Some of these songs were published as Jacquin's own work, with A.M.'s consent (see also K532, K549 and K562). A.M. was well paid for these ensembles.

K440   ARIA FOR SOPRANO, *In thee I hope.*   Composed for a pupil, which one not known, as a vocal exercise.

K441   VOCAL ENSEMBLE FOR THREE VOICES, *Dear Almond, where is the ribbon?*   Scored for S: T: B: strings. Written in Vienna 1783, words by A.M., and publicly dedicated to von Jacquin who, whilst walking with C.M. and A.M. picked up Constance's ribbon and refused to let her have it back until she or "little Mozart" could catch it (3).

K442   TRIO FOR PIANO AND STRINGS IN D MINOR.   Scored for piano: violin: cello. Written in Vienna towards the end of the eighties. Incomplete and finished by Anton Stadler with two further movements in G Major and D Major (22).

Anton Stadler (1753–1812), a clarinet and basset horn player. Employed in the Vienna State Orchestra. A.M. dedicated K581 and K622 to him.

K443   FUGUE IN G MAJOR.   Written in Vienna in 1782, incomplete again finished by Stadler.

K444   SYMPHONY NO 37 IN G MAJOR.   Scored for 2 oboe: 2 horn: strings. Written in Linz in November 1783, the first movement only by A.M., as an introduction to Michael Haydn's Symphony No 16 (see K425).

K445   MARCH IN D MAJOR.   Scored for 2 horn: strings. Written in Salzburg in the summer of 1780 to be added to K334 and known as *The Robinig March* (3).

K446   PANTOMIME MUSIC.   Scored for strings. Written in Vienna in February 1783 for a pantomime and Masquerade performance on 3 March 1783 in the Hofburg Assembly Rooms in Vienna. Only five of the original of at least 15 pieces survived. It was presented during the half hour interval, billed as a Masquerade, A.M. playing the part of Harlequin.

Extract letter 483, A.M. to L.M., Vienna, 12 March 1783:
"... both the play and the music of the pantomime were mine. Merk, the dancing master, was so kind as to coach us, and I must say that we played it charmingly."

K447   HORN CONCERTO NO 3 IN E FLAT.   Scored for solo horn: 2 clarinet: 2 bassoon: strings. Written in Vienna between 1784 and 1787 for the horn player Joseph Leutgeb (15).

This is the third horn concerto for Leutgeb, but there is some doubt as to when it was written, the second horn concerto see K495, the first K417 and the last K412.

K448   SONATA FOR TWO PIANOS IN D MAJOR.   Written in Vienna in November 1781 for his pupil Josepha Auernhammer and himself to play, first performing it on 23 November 1781 (24).

Extract letter 434, A.M. to L.M., Vienna, 24 November 1781:

> *"I happened to be at Auernhammer's concert yesterday ... we [the daughter]*
> *played the concerto a due [K365] and a sonata for two claviers [K448]*
> *which I had composed expressly for the occasion and which was a great*
> *success ... I send you also a sonata by von Daubrawaich, who said that he*
> *would be proud to have my sonata lying in his trunk; "I am proud of being*
> *your country man. You are doing Salzburg great credit."*

The journal of the Royal Society of Medicine June 1998 stated that A.M.'s
music could form a standard part of treatment for epilepsy. 29 patients with
severe epilepsy were played K448 while their brainwaves were measured;
23 of them showed very much reduced epileptic activity. When the sonata
finished they all reverted back to former levels. In one patient the occurrence
of epileptic brainwaves dropped from being present two thirds of the time
to only one fifth of the time. This was over some weeks, having been played
the sonata.

It has long been claimed that playing Mozart's music can make young
children more intelligent, although this has not been established on a
scientific basis.

Alfred Einstein called the sonata K448 "one of the most profound of all his
compositions".

K449   PIANO CONCERTO NO 14 IN E FLAT.   Scored for solo piano: 2 oboe:
2 horn: strings. Written in Vienna 9 February 1784 for his pupil Barbara
Babette Ployer (23).

A.M. was becoming one of the most fashionable pianists of his time in Vienna
in 1784. He wrote 6 piano concerti in 1784, K449–K451, K453, K456 and
K459, all these were used in subscription concerts.

Extract letter 503, A.M. to L.M., Vienna, 10 February 1784:

> *"I have works to compose which at the moment are bringing in money but*
> *probably will not do so later."*

Extract letter 504, A.M. to L.M., Vienna, 20 February 1784:

> *"The concerto is also in the original score and this too you may have copied,*
> *but have it done as quickly as possible and return it to me. Remember do*
> *not show it to a single soul, for I have composed it for Fraulein Ployer who*
> *paid me handsomely."*

Extract letter 506, A.M. to L.M., Vienna, 20 March 1784:

> *"The first concert on 17th March went off very well. The hall was full to*
> *overflowing; and the new concerto [K449] I played won extraordinary*
> *applause. Everywhere I go I hear praises of that concert."*

Barbara Babette von Ployer was the daughter of the Court Councillor in
Salzburg, a gifted pianist and one of A.M's favourite pupils. She played with
him many times, and A.M. dedicated K449 and K453 to her.

K450   PIANO CONCETO NO 15 IN B FLAT.   Scored for solo piano: flute:
2 oboe: 2 bassoon: 2 horn: strings. Written in Vienna 15 March 1784 and first
performed at the second subscription concert on 24 March 1784, A.M. playing
the pianoforte (23).

K451   PIANO CONCERTO NO 16 IN D MAJOR.   Scored for solo piano: flute:
2 oboe: 2 bassoon: 2 horn: 2 trumpet: 2 violin. Written in Vienna
22 March 1784 and first performed at the third subscription concert, 1 April
1784 (22).

This piano concerto was designed to play in private houses as the size of the
ensemble was specified for 12 players only.

Extract letter 508, A.M. to L.M., Vienna, 10 April 1784:

> *"Please don't be vexed that I haven't written to you for so long. Surely you*
> *can realise how much I have had to do in the mean-time! I have done myself*
> *great credit with my three subscription concerts ...I have composed two*
> *grand concertos,* [K450 and K451] *and then a quintet I* [K452] *which call*
> *forth the very greatest applause."*

Extract letter 514, A.M. to L.M.,Vienna, 26 May 1784:

> *"I really cannot choose between the two of them, but I regard them both as*
> *concertos which are bound to make the performer perspire. From the point*
> *of view of the difficulty the B Flat concerto* [K450] *beats the one in D* [K451].
> *Well, I am very curious to hear which of the three in B Flat, D or G, you and*
> *my sister prefer."*

K452   QUINTET FOR PIANO AND WINDS IN E FLAT.   Scored for
piano: oboe: clarinet: bassoon: horn. Written in Vienna 30 March
1784 and first performed on the third subscription concert 1 April
1784 (28).

Extract letter 508, A.M. to L.M., Vienna, 10 April 1784:

> *"... and then a quintet which called forth the very greatest applause: I myself consider it to be the best work I have ever composed. It is written for one oboe, one clarinet, one horn, one bassoon and the pianoforte. How I wish you could have heard it! And if I may say so how beautifully it was performed."*

Age 28 ✓

K453   PIANO CONCERTO NO 17 IN G MAJOR.   Scored for solo piano: flute: ✓ 2 oboe: 2 bassoon: 2 horn: strings. Written in Vienna 12 April 1784, the second concerto for his pupil Barbara Babette Ployer, who gave the first performance on 13 June 1784 in Dobling (33).   *2nd movement theme*

Extract letter 516, A.M. to N.M., Vienna, 21 July 1784:

> *"When you have tried over the three grand concertos [K450, K451 and K453] ... I shall be most anxious to hear which of them you like best dear sister."*

A.M. had a pet starling who was "almost able to whistle the finale" (K453). On ✓ June 4 the bird died; he buried it in the garden of his lodgings, with Masonic ceremony. A.M. later wrote "here lies a cherished fool, a starling bird, a musical starling bird, to its memory." *Maybe it was a starling who sang the entire Mozart concert at Bertramka, out-of-doors, in the woods. Not in good voice that day.*

K454   SONATA FOR PIANO AND VIOLIN IN B FLAT.   Written in Vienna 21 April 1784 for the violinist Regina Strinasacchi, and first performed by her on 29 April 1784.

Extract letter 510, A.M. to L.M., Vienna, 24 April 1784:

> *"We now have here the famous Strinasacchi from Mantua, a very good violinist. She has a great deal of taste and feeling in her playing. I am at this moment composing a sonata which we are going to play together on Thursday at her concert in the theatre."*

Regina Strinasacchi (1764–1839), a celebrated and famous violinist, was a student at the Ospedale della Pieta (the famous orphanage of Vivaldi in Venice). A.M. greatly admired her playing and although he was also a highly gifted violinist she was "better than I". He dedicated K454 to her.

A.M. picked up a violin at the age of 5 and astounded his father by being able to play it immediately without any lessons. He always contended that he was not a violinist (his instrument being the piano), but his violin concertos must say otherwise.

K455   VARIATIONS FOR PIANO IN G MAJOR.   Based on a theme from Gluck's *Pilgrim von Mekka*. Written in early 1783 and first performed by A.M. on 23 March 1783 (15).

Christoph Gluck (1714–1787) was Chapel Master to Maria Theresa in 1754, before going to live in Vienna in 1780 where he met A.M. He was a highly successful opera composer with over a hundred operas and greatly influenced A.M., Haydn and Beethoven.

K456   PIANO CONCERTO NO 18 IN B FLAT.   Scored for solo piano: flute: 2 oboe; 2 bassoon: 2 horn: strings. Written in Vienna 30 September 1784 for Maria Theresia von Paradies (29).

Extract letter 523, L.M. to N.M., Vienna, 16 February 1785:
> *"... on Sunday evening your brother played a glorious concerto which he had composed for Mlle. Paradies for Paris. I was sitting only two boxes away from the very beautiful Princess of ...* [he does not say who the princess is] *and had the great pleasure of hearing so clearly all the interplay of the instruments that for shear delight tears came into my eyes When your brother left the platform the Emperor* [Joseph II] *waved his hat and called out 'Bravo Mozart' and then when he came on to play, there was a great deal of clapping."*

Maria Theresia von Paradies (1759–1824) was blind from an early age (the Bernard Daskellie of her age). She was a pupil of Saleri and became a famous piano virtuoso, touring Europe, and was well known in London. K456 was written especially for her to play in Paris, but not dedicated to her. Dr Mesmer treated her but made her worse.

K457   SONATA FOR PIANO IN C MINOR.   Written in Vienna 14 October 1784 and dedicated to Maria Theresia von Trattner (18).

Extract letter 537, L.M. to N.M., Munich, 15 February 1786:
> *"I really think that Heinrich* [Marchand, L.M.'s piano pupil] *must have practised extremely hard for you will be surprised when you hear him play your brother's Fantasia and sonata* [K457]. *He played them on a fortepiano so excellently that I was thrilled."*

Maria Theresia van Trattner (1758–1793). The daughter of a celebrated mathematician and wife of a Viennese bookseller. A.M. lived in their house in 1784 and she was his student. Subscription concerts were held in the

Trattner's house in the Trattnerhof. The two families were very friendly; Maria had ten children, only one of them reaching adulthood and she was the godmother to four of A.M.'s children (six, two survived to adulthood, see K504). She died 35 years old in childbirth.

K458   STRING QUARTET IN B FLAT, *The Hunt.*   Written in Vienna 9 November 1784, the fourth of the Haydn quartets. Known as *The Hunt* due to its opening being in 6/8 time (28).

Extract letter 523, L.M. to N.M., Vienna, 16 February 1785:
> *"On Saturday evening Herr Joseph Hadyn came to see us and the new quartets were performed, or rather the three new ones [K458, K464, K465] … Hadyn said to me 'before God and as an honest man I tell you that your son is the greatest composer known to me either in person or by name'"* [see K387].

K459   PIANO CONCERTO NO 19 IN F MAJOR.   Scored for solo piano: flute: 2 oboe: 2 bassoon: 2 horn: strings. Written in Vienna 11 December 1784 for A.M. to play himself. Known as the *Second Coronation Concerto* as he played it on the 15 October 1790 in celebration of the coronation of Leopold II in Frankfurt. He also played K537 at the same concert known as the *First Coronation Concerto* (25).

K460   VARIATIONS FOR PIANO IN A MAJOR.   Two variations from Sarti's opera *Come un Agnello*. Written in Vienna in June 1784, showing a further eight variations but these are doubtful (9).

K461   SIX MINUETS FOR ORCHESTRA; C Major, E Flat, G Major, B Flat, F Major.   Written in early 1784, and the sixth minuet in D Major written in Vienna in 1786. All scored for 2 oboe/flute: 2 bassoon: 2 horn: 2 violin: bass (10).

K462   SIX CONTADANCES FOR ORCHESTRA; C Major, E Flat, B Flat, D Major, B Flat, F Major.   Scored for 2 oboe: 2 horn: 2 violin: bass. Written in Vienna in January 1784, the wind instruments added later when published by Artaria in January 1789 together with K534 and K535 (10).

K463   TWO MINUETS WITH CONTRADANCES FOR ORCHESTRA IN F MAJOR AND B FLAT, known as the *Two Quadrilles.*   Scored for 2 oboe: bassoon: 2 horn: 2 violin: bass. Written in Vienna early in 1783.

Extract letter 479, A.M. to L.M., Vienna, 22 January 1783:

> *"Last week I gave a ball in my own rooms, but of course the Chapeaux each paid two gulden. We began at six o'clock in the evening and kept on till seven. What! Only an hour? Of course not, I meant until seven o'clock next morning."*

A.M. loved to dance and wrote a great deal of dance music, a lot of it extemporised and therefore not surviving. There are 25 separate K's for dance music.

K464   STRING QUARTET IN A MAJOR.   Written in Vienna 10 January 1785, the fifth of the Haydn quartets (37).

K465   STRING QUARTET IN C MAJOR, *The Dissonance*.   Written in Vienna 14 January 1785, the sixth and last of the Haydn Quartets. The opening slow movement has strange harmonies, hence its name *The Dissonance*.

Extract letter 522, L.M. to N.M., Salzburg, 22 January 1785:

> *"Your brother adds that last Saturday he performed his six quartets for his dear old friend Haydn, and other good friends, and that he has sold them to Artaria for a hundred ducats."*

K466   PIANO CONCERTO NO 20 IN D MINOR.   Scored for solo piano: flute: 2 oboe: 2 bassoon: 2 horn: 2 trumpet: timpani: strings. Written in Vienna 10 February 1785, and first performed by A.M. on 11 February 1785 at the Mehlgrub casino in Vienna (30).

Extract letter, 523 L.M. to N.M., Vienna, 16 February 1785:

> *"Then we had a new and very fine concerto by Wolfgang [K466] which the copyist was still copying when we arrived, and the rondo of which your brother did not even to have time to play through, as he had to supervise the copying."*

A.M. often left to the last moment putting down on paper what he had in his head. This is an example of his method of composing; straight out of his head onto the keyboard.

Extract letter 538, L.M. to N.M., Salzburg, 23 March 1786:

> *"We had a concert yesterday; Marchand performed the concerto in D Minor which I sent you the other day. As you have the clavier part, he played it from the score and Haydn [Michael Haydn] turned over the pages for him."*

Heinrich Marchand (1769–1812) and his sister lived with L.M. in Salzburg from 1781 to 1784. A talented violinist and pianist employed by the court orchestra, also a student and colleague of L.M.'s.

age 29

K467 PIANO CONCERTO NO 21 IN C MAJOR, *Elvira Madigan.* Scored for solo piano: flute: 2 oboe: 2 bassoon: 2 horn: 2 trumpet: timpani: strings. Written in Vienna 9 March 1785 and first performed by A.M. 10 March 1785 at the Burg Theatre, Vienna, on an especially large and unique forte piano pedale. Known as the *Elvira Madigan,* as the adajio movement was used as the theme music in the Swedish film of the same name, a love story of an Army officer and a circus tight-rope walker (27).

The announcement for this concert:

"On Thursday 10th March 1785 Herr Kapellmeister Mozart will have the honour of giving at the I & R National Court Theatre a Grand Musical Concert for his benefit, at which not only a new just finished Forte piano Concerto will be played by him, but also an especially large Forte piano pedale will be used by him in improvising. The remaining pieces will be announced by the larger poster on the day itself."

This grand forte piano pedale A.M. had made for himself with a second keyboard which served him as a pedal. The instrument was made by Anton Walter. The receipts for this concert were 559 gulden, less expenses not outlined.

K468 SONG IN B FLAT, *Lied zur Gesellenreise* (The Travelling Song of Companions). Piano accompaniment, words by von Ratschky. Written in Vienna 26 March 1785. A Masonic song, its purpose to greet the brothers during a Masonic membership ceremony (2).

A.M. joined the Freemasons formally on 14 December 1784 in the lodge named "Beneficence", the master of which was a friend of his. He became a full fellow in such a ceremony as mentioned above on 7 June 1785. This opened up contacts for him both musically and financial, particularly Puchburg.

Empress Marie Theresa, crowned in 1740 and her son Joseph II, co-regent until she died in 1766, were against freemasonry, ultimately banning it in 1792, the French revolution being the catalyst for such ban.

K469 ORATORY, *Davidde Penitente.* Scored for 2 S: T: choir: 2 flute:

2 oboe: 2 clarinet: 2 bassoon: 3 trombone: timpani: strings. Written in Vienna in March 1785. Words possibly by da Ponte, but this is not certain. Some of this oratory was incorporated from the C Minor mass K427. First performance on 13 March 1785 at the I & R Theatre in Vienna for the benefit of the Society of Musicians pension fund (47).

K470   ANDANTE to a violin concerto in A Major.   Scored for solo violin: 2 oboe: 2 horn: strings. Written 1 April 1785 for the violin concerto by Viotti which is now lost.

K471   CANTATA, *die Maurerfreude* (The Joy of the Mason).   Scored for solo T: male chorus of 3 voices: 2 oboe: clarinet: 2 horn: strings. Written in Vienna 20 April 1785, the first performance was on 24 April 1785 at the "Crowned Hope" Masonic lodge in honour of its master, the inventor von Born. A.M. conducted the work on 16 September 1791 in Prague at the "Truth and Unity" Lodge (7).

K472   SONG IN G MINOR, *der Zauberer* (The Sorcerer). Piano accompaniment, words by C.F. Weisse. Written in Vienna 7 May 1785 (2).

K473   SONG IN B FLAT, *die Zufriedenhei* (Contentment, Happiness). Piano accompaniment, words by C.F. Weisse. Written in Vienna 7 May 1785 (3).

K474   SONG IN G MAJOR, *die Betrogene Welt* (The Betrayed World).   Piano accompaniment, words by C.F. Weisse. Written in Vienna 7 May 1785 (3).

These three songs were written for a choir, not known.

K475   FANTASIA FOR PIANO IN C MINOR.   Written in Vienna 20 May 1785 for Maria Theresia von Trattner, but not dedicated to her, unlike K457 (14).

K476   SONG IN G MAJOR, *das Veilchen* (The Violet).   Piano accompaniment, words by J.W. von Goethe. Written in Vienna 8 June 1785. A.M. discovered later that the words of the poem were by the boy Goethe, whose pseudonym at this time was Gleim (3).

K477   MASONIC FUNERAL MUSIC IN C MINOR, *Maurerische Trauermusik.* Scored for 2 oboe: 2 clarinet: 3 basset horn: double bass: 2 horn: strings. Written in Vienna in November 1785 for the funeral of two lodge brothers,

Sterlitz and Esterhauzy, and first performed at the Crowned Hope lodge on 17 November 1785 (6).

K478 QUARTET FOR PIANO AND STRINGS IN G MINOR. Scored for piano: violin: viola: cello. Written in Vienna 16 October 1785 and published by the firm of Hoffmeister in the winter of 1785 (29).

Extract letter 533, A.M. to Hoffmeister, Vienna, 20 November 1785:
> *"I turn to you in distress and beg you to help me out with some money, which I need very badly at the moment. Further I entreat you to endeavour to procure for me as soon as possible the thing you know about."*

Before the publication of K478 Hoffmeister sent him 2 ducats.

K479 QUARTET FOR VOICES, *Dite Almeno.* Scored for S: T: 2 B. Accompaniment 2 oboe: 2 clarinet: 2 bassoon: 2 horn: strings. Written in Vienna 5 November 1785 for the bass singer F. Bianchi and his wife to sing in his opera *La Villanella Rapita,* first performed on 28 November 1785 (5).

K480 TRIO FOR VOICES, *Mandina Amibice.* Scored for S: T: B: 2 flute: 2 oboe: 2 clarinet: 2 bassoon: 2 horn: strings. Written in Vienna 21 November 1785 and performed with K479 as above (6).

K481 SONATA FOR PIANO AND VIOLIN IN E FLAT. Written in Vienna 12 December 1785 and sent to Sebastian Winter, the former servant to L.M., who travelled with them around Europe. He was now employed by Prince von Furstenberg, who A.M. thought possible as an employer.

Extract letter 540, A.M. to Sebastian Winter, Vienna, 8 August 1786:
> *"I am therefore jotting down at the end of my letter a list of my latest compositions from which His Highness has only to choose, so that I may hasten to serve him ... if His Highness would be so gracious as to order from me every extract, a year, a certain number of symphonies, quartets and concertos for different instruments, and to promise a fixed yearly salary ... and I, being sure of that commission, should work with a greater peace of mind."*

The Prince did not offer any employment, but purchased a number of compositions for 143 ducats.

K482   PIANO CONCERTO NO 22 IN E FLAT.   Scored for solo piano: flute: 2 clarinet: 2 bassoon: 2 horn: 2 trumpet: timpani: strings. Written in Vienna 16 December 1785. Performed by A.M. at one of his subscription concerts in December 1785 (34). *John O'Connor recording — Irish conductor: Maelovis*

age 29

Extract letter 536, L.M. to N.M., Salzburg, 13 January 1786.

> *"I have had only one reply from your brother dated December 28th, in which he said that he gave without much preparations three subscriptions to 120 subscribers and that he had composed for this purpose a new piano concerto in E Flat, in which (a rather unusual occurrence!) he had to repeat the andante."* ! *I don't know why. For me it's over long and wanders. 1st + 3rd movements are*

K483   SONG IN B FLAT, *der Fliesset Heut*.   A three-part male chorus with organ, words by A.V. von Schlittersberg, who was a civil servant and fellow mason. Written in Vienna at the end of 1785 (2). *heavenly*

K484   SONG IN G MAJOR, *Ihr Unsere Neuen Leiter* (Our New Conductor). A three part male chorus with organ, words by A.V. von Schlittersberg. Written in Vienna at the end of 1785; both it and K483 were Masonic music and were first performed on 14 January 1786 in celebration of the first meeting of the Masonic lodge "New Crowned Hope" (3).

K485   RONDO FOR PIANO IN D MAJOR.   Written in Vienna 10 January 1786 for his pupil Wurben. The theme of this rondo is from J.C. Bach's quintet opus 11 (7).

K486   OPERA, *Impresario*.   Comic opera (Singspiel). Scored for 2 S: T: B: 2 flute: 2 oboe: 2 clarinet: 2 bassoon: 2 horn: 2 trumpet: timpani: strings. Written in Vienna 3 February 1786 in one act. Libretto by Gottlieb Stephanie, commissioned by Joseph II for a visit to Vienna of the Governor General of the Austrian Netherlands and first performed in his honour on 7 February 1786 in the Orangery of the Schonburm Palace. The concert also included an opera by Salieri (50).

K487   TWELVE DUOS FOR BASSET HORN.   Written in Vienna 27 July 1785 (20).

K488   PIANO CONCERTO NO 23 IN A MAJOR.   Scored for solo piano: flute: 2 clarinet: 2 bassoon: 2 horn: strings. Written in Vienna 2 March 1786 for A.M. to play at one of his concerts (25).

Extract letter 541, A.M. to Sebastian Winter, Vienna, 30 September 1786:

> *"But the compositions which I keep for myself or for a small circle of music-lovers and connoisseurs … there are 2 clarinets in the A Major concerto [K488], should His Highness not have any clarinets at his court, a competent copyist might transpose the parts into the suitable keys in which case the first part should be played by a violin and the second by a viola."*

K489   DUET FOR SOPRANO AND TENOR, *Spiegarti non Possio.*   Scored for S: T: 2 oboe: 2 bassoon: 2 horn: strings. Written in Vienna 10 March 1786 to be included in *Idomeneo* (K366) as a love duet added to act three for the tenor Pulini and the soprano Anna von Pufendorf, and first performed with this duet included in the private theatre of Prince Auersperg on 13 March 1786 (2).

K490   SCENA AND RONDO FOR SOPRANO (or tenor), *Non Piu Tutti.* Scored for solo S or T: 2 clarinet: 2 bassoon: 2 horn: solo violin: strings. Written in Vienna 10 March 1786 and also performed on 13 March 1786 (see above). A.M conducting. Both these additions are now regularly included in *Idomeneo* (8).

K491   PIANO CONCERTO NO 24 IN C MINOR.   Scored for solo piano: flute: 2 oboe: 2 clarinet: 2 bassoon: 2 horn: 2 trumpet: timpani: strings. Written in Vienna 24 March 1786 and performed by A.M. on 7 April 1786 at the Burg Theatre, Vienna. This concerto was only sketched out in rough as time did not allow before the concert. At the concert he improvised, and then wrote out the scoring in full afterwards (31). (See also K466.)

K492   LA NOZZE DI FIGARO, *The Marriage of Figaro*, or Figaro's Wedding. Scored for 5 S: 1 or 2 T: 3 or 4 B: chorus: 2 flute: oboe: 2 clarinet: 2 bassoon: 2 horn: 2 trumpet: timpani: strings. Started in October 1785, finished 29 April 1786. The first of the three great "da Ponte" operas, the two others being *Don* age 30 *Giovanni* (K527) and *Cosi fan Tutte* (K588). "The three great, or if not *the* greatest operas ever written." Bernard Shaw.

First performance on 1 May 1786 at the Berg Theatre, Vienna by command of Joseph II, A.M. conducting. His fee was 450 gulden, da Ponte's fee 250 gulden. *The Marriage of Figaro*, a play by Beaumarchais, was the basis of the libretto (174).

Extract letter 531, L.M. to N.M., Salzburg, 3 November 1785:

> *"My informant said something too about a new opera. Basta! I dare say we shall hear more about it"*

Extract letter 532, L.M. to N.M., Salzburg, 11 November 1785:

> *"At last I have received a letter of twelve lines from your brother, dated 2nd November. He begs to be forgiven, as he is up to the eyes in work at his opera* Le Nozze di Figaro.*"*

Extract letter 539, L.M. to N.M., Salzburg, 28 April 1786:

> *"*Le Nozze di Figaro *is being performed on 28 for the first time* [actually on 1st May] *... it will be surprising if it is a success, as I know that very powerful cabals have raged themselves against your brother. Salieri and his supporters will again try to move heaven and earth to down his opera ... it is on account of the very great reputation which your brother's exceptional talent and ability have won for him that so many people are plotting against him."*

The controversy surrounding Beaumarchais's play *The Marriage of Figaro* was well evident before A.M.'s opera. Joseph II wrote to an official a year before the opera's first performance:

> "I hear that the well know comedy *Le Marriagne de Figaro* is said to have been purposed ... in a German translation, since this piece contains so much that is objectionable (that offended the aristocratic way of life) therefore I expect that the censor shall either reject it altogether, or at any rate have such alterations made in it, that he therefore shall be responsible for the performance of this play and for the impressions it may make."

It was to have been performed as a straight play by Schihaneder's company on 3 February 1785 but this was cancelled on orders of the censor:

> "... the comedy *The M of F* was not performed yesterday ... the censorship has authorised it to be printed but not performed."

The play had been a great success in Paris as the servants get the better of their masters, hence its appeal; this was four years before the French Revolution. However A.M. and da Ponte go ahead and its first performance, having been postponed for four days, was on the 1 May 1786 in the Burgtheatre, Vienna. "One looks forward to an opera which Herr Mozart is said to have written."

Announcing the opera by advertisement on posters:
> "A new opera will be performed today for the first time. The libretto, Italian and German ... tickets at 20 Kr, performance begins at 6.30 o'clock sharp."

A.M. directed the first two performances from the harpsichord. At the second performance five arias had to be repeated, at the third performance seven arias were repeated.

From da Ponte's preface to the libretto:
> "I did not make a translation of this excellent comedy by Beaumarchais, rather an adaption, or an extract, reducing the sixteen characters down to eleven, two of whom may be performed by a single person ... In spite of every effort and diligence and care taken by the composer and myself to be brief, the opera will not be one of the shortest." (Average playing time 174 minutes.)

Critic of the first performance from Count Zinzendorf:
> "... at 7-o-clock (in fact half an hour late) to the opera *Le Nozze di Figaro*, poetry by di Ponte, music by Mozhard ... Louise in our box but even so the opera bored me."

A further detail from a critic of the first performance:
> "Storace (Susanna) the beautiful singer enchanting eye, ear and soul. Mozart directed the orchestra, playing his fortepiano; but the joy which this music causes is so removed from all sensuality, that one simply cannot speak of it ... where could words be found that are worthy to deserve such joy?"

Advertisement in the *Vienna Zeitung*, 3 May 1786:
> "... since I am so fortunate as to be able to supply to the highly estimable public with this beautiful as well as ingenious work by the celebrated Herr Kappelmeister Mozart, I did not any longer wish to with hold the news from the respected lovers of music that the score of the whole of this magnificent opera is to be had to order ... those who wish to process this opera in one form or another (full MS, quartet or piano) are therefore requested to enter their names in good time."

The publisher was Christopher Torricella.

Further in the *Vienna Zeitung*, undated:
> "... the opera by the celebrated Kappl. Herr W.A. Mozart received with such general applause, carefully arranged to be sung at the pianoforte – 7 Kr. Per sheet."

A further critic:

> "... on Monday 1st May was performed, what is not allowed to be said these days, but is sung, one may say with *Figaro*. This piece which was prohibited in Paris and not allowed to be performed here as a comedy either in a bad or a good translation, we have at least had the felicity to see represented here as an opera. It will be seen that we are doing better than the French. Herr Mozart's music was generally admired by connoisseurs already at the first performance ... the public however (this often happens to the public) did not really know on the first day how it stood. It heard many a bravo from the unbiased but obstreperous louts in the upper most stories exerted the hired lungs with all their might to deafen singers and audience alike with their St ... and Pff.. and consequently opinions were divided at the end of the piece. But now after several performances one would be subscribing to the cabals or tastelessness if one were to maintain that Herr Mozart's music is anything but a masterpiece of art. It contains so many beauties and such a wealth of ideas as can only be drawn from the source of innate genius."

A memo from Joseph II to Rosenburg:

> "... to prevent the excessive duration of the opera ... I deem the enclosed notice to the public: that no piece for more than a single voice is to be repeated. You will therefore cause some posters to this effect to be printed."

Extract letter 543, L.M. to N.M, Salzburg, 12 January 1787:

> *"His opera* Le Nozze di Figaro *was performed there* [Prague] *with such a success that the orchestra and a company of distinguished connoisseurs and lovers of music sent him letters inviting him to Prague."* [*Don Giovanni* (K527) was the result of this invitation.]

Extract letter 544, A.M. to his pupil von Jacquin, Prague, 16 January 1787:

> *"I looked on however with great pleasure while all these people flew about in sheer delight to the music of my* Figaro *arranged for contradances and German dances for here they talk about nothing but* Figaro. *Nothing is played sung or whistled but* Figaro. *No opera is drawing like* Figaro, *nothing, nothing but* Figaro. *Certainly a great honour for me!"*

Extract letter 590, A.M. to C.M., Mannheim, 23 October 1790:

> *"Dearest, most beloved little wife of my heart! It is* Figaro *which is responsible for my being here still, for the whole cast implored me to stay on and help them with their rehearsals.* Figaro *too is the reason why I cannot write to you as I would like to, as it is just the time for the dress rehearsal."*

K493   QUARTET FOR PIANO AND STRINGS IN E FLAT.   Scored for piano: violin: viola: cello. Written in Vienna 3 June 1786 (32).

Extract letter 557, A.M. to N.M., Vienna, 2 August 1788:
> *"I should very much like Haydn* [Michael] *to lend me for a short time his two Tutti-Masses ... It is now exactly a year and invited him to come and stay with me but he has not replied ... Invite him to your house at St Gilgen and play to him some of my latest compositions I am sure he will like the quartet* [K493]. *Adieu dearest sister. As soon as I can collect some new music I shall send it to you."*

K494   RONDO FOR PIANO IN F MAJOR.   Written in Vienna 10 June 1786 and expanded in January 1788 to form a sonata (K533). A.M. wrote this rondo in part payment of the debt to his friend and publisher Hoffmeister, therefore known as the *Hoffmeister Rondo* (7).

K495   HORN CONCERTO NO 4 IN E FLAT.   Scored for solo horn: 2 oboe: 2 horn: strings. Written in Vienna 26 June 1786 for Joseph Leutgeb (the cheesemonger) (see K412) (17).

K496   TRIO FOR PIANO VIOLIN AND CELLO IN G MAJOR.   Written in Vienna 8 July 1786. The piano part was written in red to remind himself not to neglect the violin and cello parts as these were written at a later date (32).

K497   PIANO SONATA FOR FOUR HANDS IN F MAJOR on one piano. Written in Vienna 1 August 1786 (27).

K498   TRIO FOR PIANO CLARINET AND VIOLA IN E FLAT, *Skittle-ground trio.*   Written in Vienna 5 August 1786 especially for the von Jacquin family, Francisca on the piano, A.M. on the viola and Anton Stadler on the clarinet, A.M. playing skittles while composing. (22).

K499   STRING QUARTET IN D MAJOR, *The Hoffmeister Quartet.*   Written in Vienna 19 August 1786 for Hoffmeister, who published it late 1786 (28).

K500   VARIATIONS FOR PIANO IN B FLAT.   Written in Vienna 12 September 1786, but some doubt as to the origin of this work (11).

K501   VARIATIONS FOR PIANO DUET IN G MAJOR.   Written in Vienna 4 November 1786 for the piano playing sisters Babette and Marianne Natorp, in five variations. The Labeque sisters of their day.

K502   TRIO FOR PIANO, VIOLIN AND CELLO IN B FLAT (30).

K503   PIANO CONCERTO NO 25 IN C MAJOR.   Scored for solo piano:
flute: 2 oboe: 2 bassoon: 2 horn: 2 trumpet: timpani: strings. Written in
Vienna 4 December 1786 for the projected series of four advent concerts
to be played in the Trattnerhof Hall, and probably first performed there
on 5 December 1786, but there is no definite documentary evidence
that these four concerts actually took place. Piano concerto no. 25
is always considered the "most difficult to play of all the concertos".
(Einstein) (31).

K504   SYMPHONY NO 38 IN D MAJOR, *The Prague* in three movements.
Scored for 2 flute: 2 oboe: bassoon: 2 horn: 2 trumpet: timpani: strings.
Written in Vienna 6 December 1786 and then taken to Prague, where A.M.
conducted its first performance on 19 January 1787 at the Prague Opera
House. Also improvising variations on the piano from *Figaro*, "the theatre
had never been so full as on this occasion". (32).

Prague newspaper, 12 January 1787:

> "... last night our great and beloved composer Herr Mozard arrived here
> from Vienna. We do not doubt that in honour of this man Herr Bondini will
> have performed *The Marriage of Figaro* this well loved work of his musical
> genius, our famous orchestra will then not fail to give new proofs of its art,
> and the discerning inhabitants of Prague will merely assemble in large
> numbers."

They did so on 19 January.

On 18 January 1787 an application to hold a musical concert is granted from
the Governor of Bohemia's office and on 19 January he performed the Prague
Symphony.

Prague newspaper, 21 January 1787:

> "On Friday 19 Herr Mozard gave a concert on the fortepiano in our
> national theatre. Everything that was to be expected of this great artist ...
> fulfilled to perfection."

Cramner's music magazine, 29 January 1787:

> "Mozart started a few weeks ago, a musical tour to Prague, Berlin, and it is
> said, even to London. I hope it will turn out to be to his advantage and
> pleasure. He is the most skilful and best keyboard player I have ever heard;

the pity is only that he aims too high in his artful and truly beautiful ?
compositions."

The second visit to London did not materialise; A.M. had been invited to go
but could not find anybody to look after their second born son Carl Thomas
(1784–1855). A.M. asked L.M. to do so but his father was ill and indeed died
in May 1787. Karl Thomas had some musical ability, taught music and was
unmarried. The second surviving son Franz Zavier Wolfgang (1791–1844)
was a civil servant, married but no children.

K505   ARIA AND SCENE FOR SOPRANO, *Chi io mi Scordi de te.*   Scored
for solo S: 2 clarinet: 2 bassoon: 2 horn: piano: strings. Written in Vienna
26 December 1786 for Anna Nancy Storace. "A declaration of love" (7).

Anna Nancy Storace (1765–1817) was a leading soprano from a musical
family who lived in Vienna from 1783–1787; she was very unhappily married
to the violinist John Fisher, and A.M. became her confidant.

K506   SONG IN F MAJOR, *Lied der Freiheit.*   Piano accompaniment; written
in Vienna at the end of 1785, the words by J.A. Blumauer. A Masonic song for
the "Truth Lodge" (2).

K507   CANON IN F MAJOR, *Cheerfulness, Frivolity.*   Written in Vienna
3 June 1786 (1).

K508   CANON IN F MAJOR, *Here's to You.*   A drinking song.   Written in
Vienna 3 June 1786 (1).

K509   SIX GERMAN DANCES; D Major, G Major, E Flat, F Major, A Major
and C Major.   Scored for 2 flute/piccolo: 2 flute: 2 oboe: 2 clarinet:
2 bassoon: 2 horn: 2 trumpet: timpani: 2 violin: bass. Written in Prague
6 February 1787 for Count Johann Pachta, a devoted music lover and
supporter of A.M. whilst in Prague (17).

K510   NINE CONTRADANCES.   Scored for 2 piccolo: 2 oboe/flute:
2 clarinet: 2 horn: 2 trumpet: timpani: 2 violin: bass. Written, probably in
Prague, in early 1787 for Pachta, but this is not authenticated.

K511   RONDO FOR PIANO IN A MINOR.   Written in Vienna 11 March
1787, influenced by the music of C.P.E. Bach (11).

K512   RECITATIVE AND ARIA FOR BASS, *Alcandro, lo Confesso.*   Scored
for flute: 2 oboe: 2 bassoon: 2 horn: strings. Written in Vienna 19 March 1787
on a text from Metastasio for the bass singer J.I.L. Fischer and first performed
by him on 21 March 1787, at the Karntnertor Theatre in Vienna (7).

Johann Fischer (1745–1825), a bass singer in the Mannheim orchestra,
having married the singer Barbara Strasser, came to Vienna where they both
had great success and sang in many of A.M.'s opera performances.

K513   ARIA FOR BASS, *Menrte ti Lascio.*   Scored for flute: 2 clarinet:
2 bassoon: 2 horn: strings. Written in Vienna 23 March 1787 for the bass
Gottfried von Jacquin (8).

K514   RONDO FOR HORN AND ORCHESTRA.   A second version of the
rondo in the horn concerto K412, but it seems that it was written in 1792,
after A.M.'s death, by whom unknown, but is now regularly played with the
horn concerto as above. (See Tyson, paper watermarks K412.)

K515   QUINTET FOR STRINGS IN C MAJOR.   Scored for 2 violin: 2 viola:
cello. Written in Vienna 19 April 1787 and originally intended to be dedicated
to the King of Prussia, who was a fine cellist and a possible employer to A.M.
but, as A.M. had to repay a debt, he was forced to offer K515 together with
K406 and K516 on subscription in April 1788 (see extract K406) (36).

Wiemar Newspaper, June 1788:
> "Mozart has now gone to Vienna as Imperial Kapellmeister. Any
> philosophical lover of music will regard him as a remarkable man. He was
> an extremely precocious genius, composing and playing from his ninth
> year onwards (indeed even earlier) like a true virtuoso to everyone's
> astonishment. But what is very rare is that he was not only a skilled
> musician at an unusually early age but that he matured in the happiest
> manner and on reaching man's estate continued to show steady
> development."

K516   QUINTET FOR STRING IN G MINOR.   Scored for as K515 (32).

K517   SONG IN E MINOR, *Die Alte.*   Piano accompaniment. Words by
F. von Hagedom, an amateur singer who also sang the first performance
in Vienna on 18 May 1787 (3).

K518   SONG IN F MAJOR, *Die Verschweigung* (Silence).   Words by Weisse, written in Vienna in May 1787 for Hagedom (3).

K519   SONG IN F MINOR, *Son of Separation.*   Piano accompaniment, words by K. Schmidt. Written in Vienna 23 May 1787 (6).

K520   SONG IN C MAJOR, *When is Louise getting the Letter?*   Piano accompaniment. Words by G. von Baumberg, written in Vienna 26 May 1787 for Gottfreid von Jacquim "in his room" as von Jacquim wished to pass this off as his own composition, and dedicate it to his girlfriend Fraulein von Altomonte (2).

K521   PIANO SONATA FOR FOUR HANDS IN C MAJOR.   Written in Vienna 29 May 1787 for Fransisca von Jacquim, Gottfried's sister, and dedicated to Babette and Marieanne Natorp (see K501). Babette later married Gottfreid's brother Julius (25).

Extract letter 547, A.M. to Baron Gottfried von Jacquim, Vienna, 29 May 1787:
> *"Please be so good as to give this sonata to your sister with my compliments and tell her to tackle it at once, for it is rather difficult. Adieu, your true friend Mozart."*

K522   DIVERTIMENTO IN F MAJOR.   Scored for 2 horn: strings: and musikalischer spass, specified as a solo violin. Written in Vienna 14 June 1787 *a age 31* as a musical joke, as the harmonic and rhythmic mistakes are purposely written to parody the work of an incompetent composer and the clumsiness of some performers. Why or to whom this was written is not known but it was composed immediately after the death of L.M. (28 May 1787) who had suggested a piece of music like this, and A.M. remembered his unfulfilled promise too late (22).

K523   SONG IN F MAJOR, *An Evening Feeling.*   Piano accompaniment. Words by J.H. Campe, written in Vienna 24 June 1787 (5).

K524   SONG IN E FLAT, *Ah, Chloe.*   Piano accompaniment. Words by J.G. Jocob written in Vienna 24 June 1787 (3).

K525   DIVERTIMENTO IN G MAJOR, *Eine kliene Nachtmusik.*   Light night music. In four movements, originally in five the second lost. Scored for

2 violin: viola: cello: bass, but in the nineteenth century transposed for a full orchestra, it is not known why or by whom. Written in Vienna 10 August 1787 as a quintet, A.M. removing the second movement to correct the form of a quintet. There is a certain mystery about this work; it is not known to whom it was written, why or when first performed, but it is likely he wrote it for himself to satisfy "an inner need" and as a corrective exercise to K522, and as a break from the second act of *Don Giovanni*. It has been described as "supreme mastery in the smallest possible frame" (Einstein) (26).

K526 SONATA FOR PIANO AND VIOLIN IN A MAJOR.   Written in Vienna 24 August 1787, often known as the *Mozart Kreutzer Sonata* and a fore-runner of the Beethoven's *Kreutzer Sonata*.

K527 DON GIOVANNI, OPERA, *Dramma Giocoso*; a jocular drama and opera buffa in two acts.   Scored for 3 S: T: 4 B: chorus: 2 flute: 2 oboe: 2 clarinet: 2 bassoon: 2 horn: 2 trumpet: 3 trombone: timpani: mandolin: strings. Commissioned by Pasquale Bondine, the Prague theatre manager, in January 1787 with an advance fee of 100 ducats. The second of the great da Ponte operas. First performance conducted by A.M. on 29 October 1787 in the National Theatre, Prague. The first performance was initially planned for the 14 October but A.M. had not finished "The Don" so instead *Figaro* was performed. The overture was written in a "great rush" on the evening before the first performance, but as there was no time to copy it out for the orchestra, it was not played until the second performance (180).

Extract letter 550, A.M. to Baron Gottfried von Jacquin, Prague, 15 October 1787:

> *"You probably think that my opera is over by now. If so, you are a little mistaken. In the first place the stage personnel here are not as smart as those in Vienna, when it comes to mastering an opera of this kind in a very short time. Secondly, I found on my arrival that so few preparations and arrangements had been made that it would have been absolutely impossible to have produced it on the 14th, that is yesterday. So yesterday my* Figaro *was performed in a fully lighted theatre and I myself conducted."*

From Prague journal, 6 October 1787:

> "Our celebrated Herr Mozart has again arrived in Prague and the news has spread here that the opera newly written by him will be given for the first time at the National Theatre."

8 October 1787, same journal:

> "The I & R poet Herr Abbe Laurenz da Ponte, a Venetian by birth , has arrived here from Vienna and will remain here for a few days. Long life to da Ponte, long live Mozart – every impresario, every virtuoso must bless them! As long as they live, it shall never be known what theatrical misery means."

A.M. stayed in Prague with the Duschek family at the Villa Bertramka, their country seat at Smichou, a suburb of Prague. The villa is now a museum and the hut in the garden where the overture was written in such great haste the evening before the first performance is now a famous Prague landmark.

Franz Zavier Duschek (1731–1799) was a pianist, a composer and teacher of great note in Prague; he married one of his students, Josepha Hambacher, and the Villa Bertramka was purchased from his concert earnings.

Critic of the first performance:

> "On Monday 29th the Italian opera company gave the ardently awaited opera by Maestro Mozard *Don Giovanni*; connoisseurs and musicians say that Prague has never yet heard the like. Herr Mozard conducted in person; when he entered the orchestra he was received with three-fold cheers, which again happened when he left it. The opera is moreover extremely difficult to perform and everyone admired the good performance given in spite of this, after such a short period of study. Everyone on the stage and in the orchestra strained every nerve to thank Mozard by rewarding him with a good performance."

A further critic of the first performance:

> "*Don Giovanni* was performed for the first time, music by Herr Mozard and was welcomed joyously and jubilantly by the numerous gathering.
> 'When Mozard's masterly music plays,
> And gathers individual praise
> The quire of Muses stays to hear
> Apollo is himself all ears.' "

Extract letter 551, A.M. to Baron Gottfried von Jacquin, Prague, 4 November 1787:

> "*My opera* Don Giovanni *had its first performance on October 29th and was received with the greatest of applause. It was performed yesterday, for the forth time entirely for my benefit.*"

The first performance of "The Don" in Vienna was on 7 May 1788 and repeated 15 times that year. He was paid 225 gulden by The Viennese Court Theatre for this revival.

A critic on this revival:
> "7 May, to the opera, *Don G* ... Mozart's music agreeable and very varied."

A further critic, 15 May:
> "In the last few days a new opera composed by Mozart has been given, but I was told it did not have much success."

Joseph II to Rosenberg, 16 May:
> "Mozard's music is certainly too difficult for the singers."

Zinzendorf's diary, 12 May 1788:
> "To the opera *Don G* was very much bored at this opera."

Count Zinzendorf's diary was an extensive record of life in Vienna in the 1780's. He was a negative and pessimistic critic of A.M.'s music but nevertheless attended "The Don" six times during 1788.

On the 31 January 1789 the opera was performed in the National Theatre, Mainz.

A critic in a Frankfurt journal:
> "On the 31st comic opera in three acts from the Italian. Music by W. Mozart. A new piece in which everyone's expectations were aroused beforehand by the composers name, and which however it thoroughly failed to please. But then the piece is in the highest degree "jejune" ['empty, thin, dry, arid, sterile', *Oxford English Dictionary*], and tedious; and Mozart's writing nearly always difficult and ingeniously wrought, seems particularly in this opera to defeat the power of assimilation of the ordinary dilettanti, majestic or humorous though it be in individual passages, and full of strong harmony as a whole."

And then again 13 March 1789:
> "*Don Juan*, Singspiel in 2 acts, freely adapted from the Italian; music by Mozart. Another opera that has turned the heads of our public. They were within an inch of storming the theatre because the doors had not been opened three hours before the beginning ... much pomp and noise from the general public; insipid and jejune. Stuff for the educated section, the music too, although great and harmonious is difficult and artificial rather than pleasing and popular."

This was the general opinion of most critics of A.M.'s operas at this time. There was tremendous musical snobbery. Jejune was the favourite word, that is why the *Magic Flute* (K620) was such a success as it appealed to the masses and not to the snobbish upper classes who thought it beneath them to appreciate popular music.

Extract letter 586, A.M. to C.M., Frankfurt, 3 October 1790:

> *"I stay indoors in my hole of a bedroom and compose ... this is the way I should like best to go on living – but – I fear that it will soon come to an end, and that I am in for a restless life ... on Tuesday the theatrical company of the Elector of Mainz are performing Don Giovanni in my honour."* [14 months to live.]

The performance did not take place but *Figaro* (K492) was performed for his benefit.

Critic from the National Theatre Manheim, 26 March 1791:

> "We at last saw again, after a long time, the Singspeil *Don Juan*; which gives such extraordinary pleasure owing to Mozart's glorious music. My musical knowledge is too restricted for me to venture on an extensive criticism of his music. It frankly carries me away, and gives me the leverist pleasure; whenever I hear it I discover some new beauty in it ... I went to hear this musical drama in which to my mind the eye was feasted, the ear enchanted, reason offended, modesty outraged, and virtue and sensibility trampled upon by vice ... never has the art of music reached to a higher degree.

K528   ARIA AND SCENE FOR SOPRANO, *Bella mia Fiamma* (My beautiful Flame).   Scored for solo S: flute: 2 oboe: 2 bassoon: 2 horn: strings. Written in Prague 3 November 1787 for Josepha Duschek, particularly to show the range and depth of her voice. This is a very difficult aria to sing (9).

K529   SONG IN F MAJOR, *Little Freddie's Birthday*.   Piano accompaniment written in Prague 6 November 1787 for little Freddie, a child of one of his friends (3).

K530   SONG IN E FLAT, *A Vision*.   Piano accompaniment, written in Prague 6 November 1787, words by L.H. Holty, for Gottfried von Jacquin (4).

Extract letter 551, A.M. to von Jacquin, Prague, 9 November 1787:

> *"... it has been a most pleasant surprise to receive your second letter. If the song [K530] in question is necessary to prove my friendship for you, you*

have no further cause to doubt it, for here it is. But I trust that even without this song you are convinced of my true friendship and in this hope I remain ever your most sincere friend. W.A.M."

K531   SONG IN C MAJOR, *Die Kleine Spinneri* (The Little Spinner Piano). Accompaniment written in Vienna, 11 December 1787 (1).

K532   TRIO FOR VOICES AND ORCHESTRA, *Glazie Aglinganni Tuoi.* Scored for S: T: B: flute: clarinet: 2 horn: 2 bassoon: bass. Written in Vienna in 1787, words by Metastasio.

K533   PIANO SONATA. Allegro in F Major, Andante in B Flat.   Written in Vienna 3 January 1788 to be added to the rondo K494 (24).

K534   CONTRADANCE FOR ORCHESTRA IN D MAJOR.   Scored for piccolo: 2 oboe: 2 horn: military side drum: 2 violin: bass. Written in Vienna 14 January 1788.

K535   CONTRADANCE FOR ORCHESTRA IN C MAJOR.   Scored for piccolo: 2 clarinet: bassoon: trumpet: military side drum: 2 violin: bass. Written in Vienna 23 January 1788 and known as the *Seige of Belgrade* (2).

K536   SIX GERMAN DANCES FOR ORCHESTRA; C Major, G Major, B Flat, D Major, F Major and F Major.   Scored for piccolo: 2 flute: 2 oboe/clarinet: 2 bassoon: 2 horn: trumpet: timpani: 2 violin: bass. Written in Vienna 27 January 1788 (see also K567) (4).

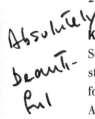

K537   PIANO CONCETO NO 26 IN D MAJOR, *The Coronation Concerto.* Scored for solo piano: flute: 2 oboe: 2 bassoon: 2 horn: 2 trumpet: timpani: strings. Written in Vienna 24 February 1788, and first performed 14 April 1789 for the Elector of Saxony in Dresden. Known as the *Coronation Concerto*, as A.M. played it on 15 October 1790 during the festivities of the coronation of Leopold II (see K459).

All the wind and brass section and most of the timpani section were not written down, and had to be extemporised; no cadenzas. The bass line of the piano (left hand) of the first and second movements missing in the certified autograph and the slow second movement only 16 bars extant (33).

Extract letter 562, A.M. to C.M., Dresden, 16 April 1789:

> *"The next day 14 April I played at court my new concerto in D, and on the following morning Wednesday 15 I received a very handsome snuff box."*

In the snuff box was 100 ducats.

Extract letter 588, A.M. to C.M., Frankfurt, 15 October 1790:

> *"My concert took place at 11 o'clock this morning* [played K537 and K459], *it was a splendid success from the point of view of honour and glory but a failure as far as money was concerned. I must close this letter or I shall miss the post. Moreover I seem to notice that you doubt my punctuality or rather my eagerness to write to you, and this pains me bitterly. Surely you ought to know me better. Good God! Only love me half as much as I love you, and I shall be content."*

K538   ARIA FOR SOPRANO, *Ah se in Ceil.*   Scored for solo S: 2 oboe: 2 bassoon: 2 horn: strings. Words by Metastasio. Written in Vienna 4 March 1788 for his sister-in-law Aloysia Lange, who sang it in the concert interval on 7 March 1788 in the Burg Theatre, Vienna. This is the last aria he wrote for Aloysia, his emotional relationship with her finally had ended (9).

K539   ARIA FOR BASS, *How I would like to be the Emperor.*   Scored for Solo B: piccolo: 2 oboe: 2 bassoon: 2 horn: percussion: strings. Written in Vienna 5 March 1788 for the Bass Friedrich Baumann, and first performed by him on 7 March 1788 in the Leopoldstadter, Vienna. A German war song (3).

K540   ADAJIO FOR PIANO IN B MINOR.   Written in Vienna 19 March 1788; for whom, why or when it was first performed is not known. "Such a piece, without any further purpose, may simply have flowed from his pen in an hour at once tragic and blessed." Einstein (11).

K541   ARIETTA FOR BASS, *Un Bacio di Mano.*   Scored for solo B: flute: 2 oboe: 2 bassoon: 2 horn: strings. Written in Vienna in May 1788 for the Bass Albert Arelli and first performed by him in the Burg Theatre 2 June 1788. Words possibly by da Ponte, although this is not certain. The theme of this arietta was then used as the main theme in the first movement of the Jupiter Symphony (see K551) (2).

K542   TRIO FOR PIANO VIOLIN AND CELLO IN E MAJOR.   Written in Vienna 22 June 1788, dedicated to Michael Puchberg (25).

Extract letter 554, A.M. to Michael Puchberg, Vienna, before 17 June 1788:

> *"If you have sufficient regard and friendship for me to assist me for a year or two with one or two thousand gulden, at a suitable rate of interest, you will help me enormously. As to security I so not suppose that you will have any doubts. You know more or less how I stand and you know my principles … when are we to have a little musical party at your house again? I have composed a new trio* [K542]*."*

Michael Puchberg sent 200 gulden.

K543   SYMPHONY NO 39 IN D FLAT in four movements.   Scored for flute: 2 clarinet: 2 bassoon: 2 trumpet: timpani: strings. Written in Vienna 26 June 1788 for a series of subscription concerts A.M. was planning (31).

Symphonies 39, 40 and 41 (see K550 and K551) are generally considered the three most important and influential symphonies composed in the eighteenth century. These three masterpieces were written in the space of six weeks in the summer of 1788, the three dates in A.M.'s Thematic catalogue are dated 26 June, 25 July and 10 August.

By now his finances were in a precarious state.

Extract letter 553, A.M. to Michael Puchberg, Vienna, June 1788 (no precise date):

> *"Dearest brother. Your true friendship and brotherly love embolden me to ask a great favour of you. I still owe you eight ducats. Apart from the fact that at the moment I am not in a position to pay you back this sum, I dare to implore you to help me out with a hundred gulden until next week when my concerts in the Casino are to begin. By that time I shall certainly have received my subscription money* [for K543, K550 and K551]*."*

Puchberg sent another 100 gulden.

Extract letter 555, A.M. to Michael Puchberg, Vienna, 27 June 1788:

> *"I am very much distressed that your circumstances at the moment prevent you from assisting me as much as I could wish, for my position is so serious that I am unavoidably obliged to raise money somehow … during the ten days since I came to live here I have done more work than in two months of my former quarters."*

Extract letter 556, A.M. to Michael Puchberg, Vienna, beginning of July 1788:

> *"Dearest and BO* [Brother of the Order] *owing to great difficulties and*

complications my affairs have become so involved that it is of the utmost importance to raise some money on these two pawnbrokers tickets. In the name of our friendship I implore you to do me this favour; but you must do it immediately. Forgive my importunity, but you know my situation. Ah! If only you had done what I asked you! Do it even now – then everything will be as I desire. Ever your Mozart."

K544   MARCH IN D MAJOR.   Scored for flute: horn: strings. Written in Vienna in June 1788 but now lost.

K545   PIANO SONATA IN C MAJOR, *Little Sonata for Beginners.*   Written in Vienna 26 June 1788. This was written in A.M.'s catalogue. "Too easy for a child, too difficult for adults" (14).

Extract letter 557, A.M. to N.M., Vienna, 2 August 1788:
"Indeed you have every reason to be vexed with me! But will you really be so when you receive by mail coach my very latest compositions for the clavier? Surely not. This I hope, will make everything alright again. My little sonata for beginners! ... dear sister you must realise that I have a great deal to do. Besides, you know very well that I am rather lazy about letter-writing. But this must not prevent you writing very often to me. Indeed though I detest writing letters, I love getting them."

K546   ADAJIO AND FUGUE FOR STRINGS IN C MINOR.   A string quartet or for a string orchestra, for whom or why unknown. Written in Vienna 26 June 1788 originally as a string quartet, but the fugue added from K426 (6).

K547   SONATA FOR PIANO AND VIOLIN IN F MAJOR.   Written in Vienna 10 July 1788, the last sonata for the piano and the violin (19).

K548   TRIO FOR PIANO, VIOLIN AND CELLO IN C MAJOR.   Written in Vienna 14 July 1788 (22).

K549   TRIO FOR VIOLAS AND VOCAL ENSEMBLE.   Scored for 2 S: B: viola: 3 basset horns. Written in Vienna 16 July 1788, its authenticity is doubtful (2).

K550   SYMPHONY NO 40 IN G MINOR in four movements.   Scored for flute: 2 oboe: (2 clarinet) 2 bassoon: 2 horn: strings. Written in Vienna 25 July

32

1788 with a second version within the month, adding clarinet specifically for Anton Stadler (36).

Here again, as with K543 and K551, it is not certain when the first performance took place, but as clarinets were added it should be presumed that in the subscription concerts in Leipzig in 1789, in Frankfurt 1790 and in Vienna 1791 as "the latest symphonies by Mozart" that these three last symphonies were played at this time.

K551   SYMPHONY NO 41 IN C MAJOR, *The Jupiter Symphony* in four movements.   Scored for flute: 2 oboe: 2 bassoon: 2 horn: 2 trumpet: timpani: strings. Written in Vienna 10 August 1788. The name Jupiter given to this symphony by Johann Salomon 1745–1815, a German impresario and violinist, working in London in 1880–1804 with Haydn (38).

K552   SONG IN A MAJOR, *When leaving for the Field.*   Piano accompaniment written in Vienna 11 August 1788; a war song (7).

K553   CANON IN C MAJOR, *Alleluia.*   3 in 1 piano and violin accompaniment written in Vienna 2 September 1788 and based on a Gregorian chant for Easter Sunday. Three voices (3).

K554   CANON IN F MAJOR, *Ave Maria.*   4 in 1 piano and violin accompaniment written in Vienna 2 September 1788. Four voices (2).

K555   CANON IN A MINOR, *Lacrimoso son'io.*   4 in 1 piano and violin accompaniment written in Vienna 2 September 1788, with a second substitute text by Caldara (2).

K556   CANON IN G MAJOR, *Grechtelt's Eruck.*   4 in 1 piano and violin accompaniment. Written in Vienna 2 September 1788 (1).

K557   CANON IN F MINOR, *Nascoso eil mio Sol.*   4 in 1 piano accompaniment written in Vienna 2 September 1788, the original text by Caldara (2).

K558   CANON IN B FLAT, *Let's go to the Fair.*   4 in 1 piano and violin accompaniment written in Vienna 2 September 1788 (1).

K559   CANON IN F MAJOR.   3 in 1 piano and violin accompaniment written in Vienna 2 September 1788 (1).

K560   CANON IN F MAJOR, *O Peter, you Silly Donkey.*   4 in 1 written in Vienna 2 September 1788 (1).

K561   CANON IN A MAJOR, *Goodnight!*   4 in 1 written in Vienna 2 September 1788 (1).

K562   CANON IN A MAJOR, *Caro Bella mio.*   3 in 1 written in Vienna 2 September 1788 (2).

It is not known why these ten pieces were written; all in the catalogue 2 September 1788 (see K439). Songs of good fellowship for the von Jacquin's circle.

K563   DIVERTIMENTO FOR STRING TRIO IN E FLAT.   Scored for violin: viola: cello. Written in Vienna 27 September 1788 for Michael Puchberg, called a divertimento as there are two minuets in the six movements (42).

Extract letter 562, A.M. to C.M., Dresden, 16 April 1789:
>*"So we performed it in the chapel with Anton Teiber, who as you know is organist here, and with Herr Kraft, Prince Esterhazy's cellist who is here with his son. At this little concert I introduced the trio which I wrote for Herr von Puchberg and it was played quite decently* [see K581]*"*.

K564   TRIO IN G MAJOR.   Scored for piano: violin: cello. Written in Vienna 27 October 1788 "for Beginners". It was commissioned by Stephen Storance for his students, hence the easy parts for the three instruments (21).

K565   TWO CONTRADANCE IN B FLAT AND D MAJOR.   Scored for 2 oboe: 2 horn: bassoon: 2 violin: bass. Written in Vienna and specified by A.M. in his thematic catalogue 30 October 1788 but no trace of this work has ever been found.

K566   INSTRUMENTATION OF HANDEL'S ACIS AND GALATEA.   Handel originally wrote this work in 1718, the original scoring: S: 3 T: B; recorder: 2 oboe: bassoon: 2 violin: viola: basso continuo. Additional scoring by A.M: 2 flute: 2 clarinet: bassoon: 2 horn. The instrumentation written in November 1788 and first performed for A.M.'s benefit in November 1788 under his direction in the Jahn Rooms in Vienna.

This was the first of four Handel arrangements for Gottfried von Swieten, who in 1780 formed the "Society of Noblemen for the cultivation of classical music" especially for Handel's music (see also K572, K591 and K592).

K567 SIX GERMAN DANCES FOR ORCHESTRA; B Flat, E Flat, D Major, A Major, C Major. Scored for piccolo: 2 flute: 2 oboe/clarinet: 2 horn: 2 trumpet: timpani: 2 violin: bass. Written in Vienna 6 December 1788 and with K536, these 12 German dances were intended as a complete cycle, and all published by Ataria in 1789 (14).

K568 TWELVE MINUETS FOR ORCHESTRA; in C Major, F Major, B Flat, E Flat, G Major, D Major, A Major, F Major, B Flat, D Major, G Major and C Major. Scored for 2 flute/piccolo: 2 oboe/clarinet: 2 bassoon: 2 horn: 2 trumpet: timpani: 2 violin: bass. Written in Vienna 24 December 1788 (29).

K569 ARIA FOR SOPRANO, *Without constraint.* Scored for 2 oboe: 2 bassoon: 2 horn: strings. Written in Vienna, January 1789 for his sister-in-law Josepha Weber but now lost.

K570 PIANO SONATA IN B FLAT, *The Little Sonata.* Written in Vienna in February 1789 for teaching purposes. A spurious version with violin also exists (19).

K571 SIX GERMAN DANCES FOR ORCHESTRA D MAJOR; A Major, C Major, G Major, B Flat, and D Major. Scored for 2 flute/piccolo: 2 oboe/clarinet: 2 bassoon: 2 horn/trumpet: timpani: percussion: 2 violin: bass. Written in Vienna 21 February 1789 (16).

K572 INSTRUMENTATION OF HANDEL'S MESSIAH. Handel wrote *The Messiah* in 6 weeks in 1742. Original scoring: S: A: T: B: choir: 2 oboe: 2 trumpet: timpani: strings. Additional scoring in February/March 1789 by A.M.: 2 flute: 2 clarinet: 2 bassoon: 2 horn: 3 trombone. Later revised the trumpet parts. A.M. stayed with Count Johan Esterhazy and was paid by the Society of Noblemen for the Cultivation of Classical Music. The first performance on 6 March 1789.

Hand written note on the title page of a text book of *The Messiah* 6 March 1789, written by a member of the choir:

"Excellently performed on 6th March 1789 at Count Johan Esterhazy's.

Mozart directed the orchestra and the orchestration, an improvement on the original."

From Zinzendorf's diary, 7 March 1789:

"... before 7-o'clock to the concert at Jean Esterhazy's, *Der Messias*, music by Haendel. I found it a little tedious, although the music was quite beautiful. The trumpet shall sound was quite different and seemed to be heavily cut."

K573 VARIATIONS ON A MINUET FOR PIANO IN D MAJOR. The variations from a sonata by J.P. Duport, written in Potsdam on 29th April 1789 (15).

Jean-Pierre Duport (1741–1812) was appointed a cellist by Frederick the Great of Prussia. A.M. wrote this variation in nine small movements, sending it to Duport with the intention of getting employment from Frederick the Great, and although nothing came of this request, he received a commission from the King to write some string quartets for his son Prince Frederick William. The original commission was for six Prussian quartets but A.M. only completed only three (K575, K589 and K590).

K574 GIGUE FOR PIANO IN G MAJOR. Written in Leipzig 16 May 1789 as a tribute to J.S. Bach (2).

K575 STRING QUARTET IN D MAJOR, *The Prussian Quartet* Written in Vienna in June 1789, the first of the three quartets written for Prince William (see K573 above). They were published in December 1791 by Artaria (24).

Extract letter 567, A.M. to Michael Puchberg, Vienna, 12 July 1789:

"Great God! I would not wish my worst enemy to be in my present position ... dearest, most beloved friend and brother – you know my present circumstances, but you also know my prospects ... meanwhile I am composing six easy clavier sonatas for Princess Friederike, and six quartets for the King ... in a month or two my fate must be decided in every detail ... so it all depends, my only friend, upon whether you will or can lend me another five hundred gulden. Until my affairs are settled I undertake to pay back ten gulden a month ...
P.S. O God! I can hardly bring myself to dispatch this letter ... and yet I must."

Puchberg sent 150 gulden.

On 26 May 1789 A.M. played before the Court in Potsdam, receiving a gold snuff-box with one hundred gold coins in it; further the King commissioned six easy piano sonatas for his daughter and six string quartets for himself. Only three string quartets completed as above and only one piano sonata (see K576).

On 28 December 1791, three weeks after A.M. died, an advertisement appeared in the *Vienna Zeitung*:

> "From Artaria and comp. Art dealers in the Kohlmarkt are to be had ... three entirely new concert ante quartets for 2 violins, viola and cello by the late and lamented Herr Kapellmeister Mozart. These quartets are one of the most estimable works of the composer Mozart, who was torn untimely from this world; they flowed from the pen of this so great musical genius not long before his death, and they display all that musical interest in respect of art, beauty and taste which must awaken pleasure and admiration not only in the amateur but in the true connoisseur also. Care has also been taken as to their outward appearance, and this addition of these masterpieces has been prepared and printed in a clear, clean and correct type on fine and good paper – these three quartets cost three fl."

The result of this offer was a great success, as on 7 January 1792 in the same paper:

> "At the same time let it be recorded that the quartets by Herr Mozart recently published from our press and received with such general acclaim, that we have had to print more of them, may still be had for three fl."

K576   PIANO SONATA IN D MAJOR.   Written in Vienna in July 1789 for Princess Friederike. The first of the intended 6 easy sonatas for her (see letter 567). This last sonata never reached the Princess and was published posthumously (15).

K577   RONDO FOR SOPRANO, *Al Desio Ch'adora*.   Scored for 2 basset horn: 2 bassoon: 2 horn: strings. Written in Vienna in July 1789 as an additional rondo for *The Marriage of Figaro* (7).

K578   ARIA FOR SOPRANO, *Alma Grande*.   Scored for 2 oboe: 2 bassoon: 2 horn: strings. Written in Vienna August 1789 for the soprano Louise Villeneuve for her to sing in an opera by Cimarosa (4).

K579 ARIA FOR SOPRANO, *Un Moto di Gioia.*   Written in Vienna in August 1789 for the soprano Adriana Ferraresi as an additional aria for *The Marriage of Figaro*, for its performance on 29 August 1789 (1).

Extract letter 571, A.M. to C.M., Vienna, 19 August 1789:
> *"The little aria which I have just composed for Madame Ferreresi ought, I think, to be a success, provided she is able to sing it in an artless manner, which, however, I very much doubt. She herself liked it very much I have just lunched at her house. I think* Figaro *will be performed on Sunday for certain."*

K580 ARIA FOR SOPRANO.   Scored for solo S: 2 clarinet: bassoon: 2 horn: strings. Written in Vienna 17 September 1789 for his sister-in-law Josefa Weber, now Hofer, for an abandoned production of Paisiello's *Barber of Seville*.

K581 QUINTET FOR CLARINET AND STRINGS IN A MAJOR, *The Stadler Quintet.*   Scored for clarinet: 2 violin: viola: cello. Written in Vienna 29 September 1789 for the clarinettist Anton Stadler. Specified in score as a basset clarinet, a new type of clarinet with an extension of a major third. The first performance took place on the 22 December 1789 in the Berg Theatre.

Poster of this concert given by the Society of Musicians:
> "Musical concert today 22 December 1789 will be held at the Berg Theatre for the benefit of its widows and orphans. Between the two parts of this concert a new quintet by Herr Mozart will be given, in which the principal players will be Herr Stadler, court musician. The music, counting both instruments and voices will be performed by more than one hundred and eighty persons. To begin at 7-o'clock."

Extract letter 576, A.M. to Michael Puchberg, on or before 8 April 1790:
> *"But if you can extricate me from a temporary embarrassment, then, for the love of God, do so! Whatever you can easily spare will be welcome. I possible, forget my importunity and forgive me. Tomorrow, Friday, Count Hadik has invited me to perform for him Stadler's quintet* [K581] *and the trio I composed for you* [K563] *... I would have gone to see you myself in order to have a chat with you, but my head is covered with bandages due to rheumatic pains."*

Puchberg sent him 25 gulden.

K582   ARIA FOR SOPRANO, *Chisa, Chisa qual Sia*   Scored for 2 clarinet:
2 bassoon: 2 horn: strings. Written in Vienna in October 1789, text by
da Ponte, for the soprano Louise Villeneuve and first performed on
9 November1789 in the Berg Theatre (3).

K583   ARIA FOR SOPRANO, *Vado, ma Dove.*   Scored for 2 clarinet:
2 bassoon: 2 horn: strings. Written in Vienna in October 1789, text by da
Ponte, also for the concert also on 9 November (3).

K584   ARIA FOR BASS, *Rivolgete Lui lo Sguardo.*   Scored for 2 oboe:
2 bassoon: 2 trumpet: 2 timpani: strings. Written in Vienna in 1789 for the
bass singer Benucci, and later included into *Cosi Fan Tutte*. K588 was written
at the same time (7).

K585   TWELVE MINUETS FOR ORCHESTRA; D Major, F Major, B Flat, E
Flat, G Major, C Major, A Major, F Major, B Flat, E Flat, G Major and D Major.
Written in Vienna in December 1789 to be used as dance minuets for a party
being given over Christmas in the Assembly Rooms Vienna. Scored for
originally for strings but later supplemented with wind parts (29).

K586   TWELVE GERMAN DANCES FOR ORCHESTRA; C Major, G Major, B
Flat, F Major, A Major, D Major, G Major, E Flat, B Flat, F Major, A Major and
C Major.   Scored for 2 flute/piccolo: 2 oboe/ clarinet: 2 bassoon: 2 horn:
2 trumpet: timpani: percussion: 2 violin: bass. Written in Vienna in December
1789 for the same occasion as above (26).

K587   CONTRADANCE IN C MAJOR in one movement.   Scored for flute:
oboe: bassoon: trumpet: 2 violin: bass. Written in Vienna in December 1789,
again for the above occasion (2).

K588   COSSI FAN TUTTE, *Thus do all Women* (feminine fickleness).   Comic
opera in two acts. Scored for 3 S: T: 2 B:chorus: 2 flute: 2 oboe: 2 clarinet:
2 bassoon: 2 horn: 2 trumpet: strings: timpani. Commissioned by Joseph II
in November 1789, the third and last libretto by da Ponte. First performed on
26 January 1790 in the Berg Theatre, Vienna, the original fee being 200
ducats (182).

The death of Joseph II on 20 February 1790 and the accession of his brother
Leopold II halted all performances; it was revived on the 10 June 1790 for 10
performances and then rarely performed, and it is only in the past 50 years
has it become part of the standard repertory.

Although the first performance was on 26 January 1790 there was a "Little rehearsal at Mozart's on 31 December 1789 when Haydn came to listen and praise"; on 24 January 1790 a full dress orchestral dress rehearsal, again with Haydn and Puchberg present.

Extract letter 572, A.M. to Michael Puchberg, Vienna, December 1789 (no precise date):

> *"Only to you most beloved friend, who knows everything about me and my circumstances, have I the courage to open my heart completely. According to the present arrangements I am to receive from the management next month 200 duckets for my opera. If you can and will lend me 400 gulden until then, you will be rescuing your friend from the greatest embarrassment ... once more I beg you to rescue me from my horrible situation ... but then I invite you to come along on Thursday at 10-o'clock to hear a short rehearsal of my opera. I am only inviting Haydn and yourself. I shall tell you when we meet about Salieri's plots, which however have completely failed already."*

Puchberg sent 200 gulden.

Extract letter 573, A.M. to Michael Puchberg, Vienna, 20 January 1790:

> *"I am very much touched by your friendship and kindness. If you can and will send me an extra hundred gulden, you will oblige me very greatly ... we are having the first instrumental rehearsal in the theatre tomorrow, Haydn is coming with me."*

Puchberg sent 100 gulden.

Zinzendorf's diary, late evening 26 January 1790:

> "Before 7-o'clock to the new opera *Cosi fan Tutte*. The music by Mozart is charming and the subject rather amusing."

Critic from the revival of 6 June 1790:

> "I can again announce an excellent work by Mozart to you."

From Artaria Publishers:

> "For sale the best arias from the new opera ... 20 kr each."

18 scenes and 31 numbers were offered for sale with piano accompaniment.

Further critics:

> "Singspiel composed by Mozart is a miserable thing which lowers all women, cannot possibly please female spectators and therefore will not make its fortune. Love and temptation a miserable piece of work but with forceful, elevated music of A.Mozart."

K589 STRING QUARTET IN B FLAT.   The second "Prussian Quartet", written in Vienna in May 1790 (25).

K590 STRING QUARTET IN F MAJOR.   The third and last "Prussian Quartet" Written in Vienna in June 1790 (23).

Extract letter 578, A.M. to Michael Puchberg, Vienna, beginning of May 1790:

> *"I am thinking of giving subscription concerts at home during the next three months of June July and August … but I must have something to live on until I have arranged my concerts and until the quartet on which I am working have been sent to be engraved. So if only I had in hand six hundred gulden at least, I should be ably to compose with a fairly easy mind. And ah! I must have peace of mind. But what worries me dreadfully at the moment is a debt to the haberdasher … demanding payment urgently and impatiently. The debt amounts to one hundred gulden."*

Puchberg sent 100 gulden.

Extract letter 580, A.M. to Michael Puchberg, Vienna, on or before 17 May 1790:

> *"Alas I must still ask you to wait patiently for the sums I have already been owing you for such a long time. If only you knew what grief and worry all this causes me. It has prevented me all this time from finishing my quartets."*

Puchberg sent another 100 gulden on 17 May.

K591 INSTRUMENTATION OF HANDEL'S ALEXANDER'S FEAST.   Written by Handel in 1736 with original scoring S: T: B: choir: 2 recorder: 2 oboe: 3 bassoon: 2 horn: 2 trumpet: timpani: strings. A.M.'s additional instrumentation: 2 flute: 2 clarinet: revision of trumpet parts. Written in Vienna in July 1790 for von Swieten's Society of Noblemen for the Cultivation of Classical Music.

K592 INSTRUMENTATION OF HANDEL'S ODE FOR ST CECILIA'S DAY. Written by Handel in 1739 with original scoring: S: T: choir: flute: 2 oboe: 2 trumpet: timpani: lute: strings. A.M.'s additional instrumentation: flute: 2 clarinet: 2 bassoon: 2 horn: revised trumpet parts. Written in Vienna in July 1790, both these arrangements of Handel's works were performed privately in von Swieten's house, A.M. directed both of them (see also K566).

K593 STRING QUINTET IN D MAJOR.   Started in September 1790, finished end of December 1790. Commissioned by the violinist Johann Tost, who had recently married a wealthy woman; A.M. was well paid for this quintet and also for K614.

Johann Tost was a violinist in the Haydn Esterhazey Orchestra. Before Haydn's departure for London in December 1790, A.M. gave a party for him and the quintet was played by A.M., Haydn, Tost, Stadler, and a fifth member of the orchestra (30).

K594 ADAJIO AND ALLEGRO FOR MECHANICAL ORGAN IN F MINOR AND F MAJOR.   Written in Vienna and Frankfurt between October and December 1790. Commissioned by Josef Muller, the owner of a waxworks, for the opening of an exhibition of the wax effigy of Field Marshall Laudon. The mechanical organ featured was powered by a clockwork mechanism; this part is now generally played as an organ solo. See also K608 and K616 (13).

Extract letter 586, A.M. to C.M., Frankfurt, 3 October 1790:
> *"Dearest, most beloved little wife! At last I feel comforted and happy. First of all, because I have had news from you, my love, news for which I am simply aching; and secondly, on account of the reassuring information about my affairs. I have now made up my mind to compose at once the adagio for the clockmaker, and then to slip a few ducats into the hand of my dear little wife. And this I have now done. But as it is the kind of composition which I detest, I have not unfortunately been able to finish it. I compose a bit of it everyday – but I have to break off now and then as I get bored."*

K595 PIANO CONCERTO NO 27 IN B FLAT.   Scored for solo piano: flute: 2 oboe: 2 bassoon: 2 horn: strings. Written in Vienna 5 January 1791, but started in 1788 and laid aside. First performed by A.M. on 4 March 1791 at a concert arranged by Joseph Bahr, a well known clarinettist, in the Jahn Hall, Vienna (34).

The last piano concerto and the last public concert; a hand-bill announcing it:
> "Herr Bahr, chamber musician in actual service to H. Russian Imperial Majesty, will have the honour on Friday next, 4th March, to hold a grand musical concert at Herr Jahn's Hall, letting himself be heard several times … and Herr Kapellmeister Mozart will play a concerto on the pianoforte [K595]. Those who are still desirous of submitting can be provided with tickets each day at Herr Jahn's. To begin at 7-o'clock pm."

After his many public performances, unknowingly this being his last, this was an important and successful concert, as the *Vienna Zeitung* reported on 12 March 1791:

"Herr Bahr held a grand concert on 4th March ... our Mozart played a concerto on the pianoforte and everybody admired his art in composition as well as his performance."

K596   SONG IN F MAJOR, *Komar Weber Mai*.   Words by Christian Ouerbeck Written in Vienna 14 January 1791 (2).

K597   SONG IN E FLAT, *Await to the new life*.   Words by C.C. Sturm. Written in Vienna 14 January 1791 (5).

K598   SONG IN A MAJOR, *We children*.   Words by Christian Ouerbeck. Written in Vienna 14 January 1791, these three songs were published by Alberti early in 1791 with piano accompaniment (1).

K599   SIX MINUETS FOR ORCHESTRA; C Major, G Major, E Flat, B Flat, F Major and D Major.   Scored for 2 flute/piccolo: 2 oboe/clarinet: 2 bassoon: 2 horn; 2 trumpet: timpani: 2 violin: bass. Written in Vienna 23 January 1791 and published by Artaria as a series of 12 dances, together with K601 and K604 with piano and string trio versions (14).

K600   SIX GERMAN DANCES FOR ORCHESTRA; C Major, E Major, B Flat, E Flat, G Major and D Major.   Scored for piccolo: 2 flute: 2 oboe/clarinet: 2 bassoon: 2 horn: 2 trumpet: timpani: 2 violin: bass. Written in Vienna 29 January 1791 together with K602 and K605 as thirteen German dances. The fifth dance in the series is known as *The Canary*, as A.M. owned a canary, and is a mimic of the bird's singing (15).

K601   FOUR MINUETS FOR ORCHESTRA; A Major, C Major, G Major and D Major.   Scored for 2 flute/piccolo: hurdy-gurdy: 2 oboe/clarinet: 2 bassoon: 2 horn: 2 trumpet: timpani: 2 violin: bass. Written in Vienna early 1791 with K599 and K604 as twelve minuets (11).

K602   FOUR GERMAN DANCES FOR ORCHESTRA; B Flat, F Major, C Major, A Major.   Scored for 2 flute/piccolo: hurdy-gurdy: 2 oboe/clarinet: 2 bassoon: 2 horn/trumpet: timpani: 2 violin: bass. Written in Vienna 5 February 1791. The third dance is known as *Die Leyerer* (10).

K603   TWO CONTADANCES FOR ORCHESTRA; D Major, B Flat.   Scored for piccolo: 2 oboe: 2 bassoon: 2 horn: 2 trumpet: timpani: 2 violin: bass. Written in Vienna 5 February 1791 (3).

K604   TWO MINUETS FOR ORCHESTRA; B Flat, E Flat.   Scored for 2 flute: 2 clarinet: 2 bassoon: 2 trumpet: timpani: 2 violin: bass. Written in Vienna 12 February 1791 (5).

K605   THREE GERMAN DANCES FOR ORCHESTRA; D Major, G Major, C Major.   Scored for 2 flute: piccolo: 2 oboe: 2 bassoon: 2 horn/trumpet: 2 post-horn: timpani: 5 sleigh bells: 2 violin: bass. Written in Vienna 12 February 1791, the third dance known as *The Sleighride* (6) (not to be confused with L.M.'s *Sleighride*).

K606   SIX GERMAN DANCES; all in B Flat.   Scored for 2 violin: bass. The wind parts of flute: bassoon: oboe: 2 horn, originally   Scored for these dances, have now been lost, and only known to have existed on A.M's thematic catalogue. Written in Vienna 28 February 1791 (5).

K607   CONTRADANCE IN E FLAT, *Il Trionfo delle Dame*   Scored for flute: bassoon: 2 oboe: 2 horn: 2 violin: bass. Written in Vienna 28 February 1791 but not completed, as the score mysteriously breaks off (1).

K608   FANTASIA FOR MECHANICAL ORGAN IN F MINOR.   Written in Vienna 3 March 1791. There is no evidence to suggest that the commission for this work came from Josef Muller, the owner of the waxworks (see K594). Muller had the only instrument of this type in Vienna at this time and therefore it seems likely that the work was written for him, but Haydn's clockmaker (*The Clock Symphony*) Neimecz may have commissioned A.M. as he also owned a mechanical clock organ with restricted notes (13).

K609   FIVE CONTRADANCES FOR ORCHESTRA; C Major, E Flat, D Major, C Major and G Major.   Scored for flute: side-drum: 2 violin: bass. Written in Vienna either in 1791 or, possibly, earlier in 1787 (8).

K610   CONTRADANCE FOR ORCHESTRA IN G MAJOR, *The Naughty Girls.* Scored for 2 flute: 2 horn: 2 violin: bass. Written in Vienna in March 1791 (2).

K611   GERMAN DANCE IN C MAJOR.   Scored for 2 flute: hurdy-gurdy:
2 oboe: 2 bassoon: 2 trumpet: timpani: 2 violin: bass. Written in Vienna
6 March 1791, the third dance, *Die Leyerer* (K602) is also included in this
work (3).

K612   ARIA FOR BASS, *der questa Bella Mano.*   Scored for solo B: flute:
2 oboe: 2 bassoon: 2 horn: double bass solo: strings. Written in Vienna
17 March 1791 for the bass Franz Gerl and the double bass player Friedrich
Pischelberger. A.M. wrote this specifically for Gerl as a test for his voice, as
Gerl was the first Sarastro in *The Magic Flute* (7).

K613   EIGHT VARIATIONS FOR PIANO IN F MAJOR, *A woman is a
marvellous thing.*   Written in Vienna in March 1791 from a popular song
being played in Schikaneder's theatre; A.M. becoming more involved with this
successful theatre group culminating in *The Magic Flute* (see K620) (15).

K614   STRING QUINTET IN E FLAT.   Written in Vienna 12 April 1791 for
the violinist Johann Tost (see K593); first performed at a musical soirée on
14 April 1791 in Tost's house, which had a small concert room (29).

Extract letter 592, A.M. to Michael Puchberg, Vienna, 13 April 1791:
*I shall be drawing my quarterly pay on April 20th, that it is, in a week. If
you can and will lend me until then about twenty gulden, you will oblige me
very much, most beloved friend, and you will have it back with very many
thanks on the twentieth as soon as I draw my money. I am anxiously
awaiting the sum.*

Puchberg sent 30 gulden. A.M. was paid 800 gulden per annum.

K615   CHORUS, *Viviamo Felici.*   Scored for chorus. Written in Vienna
20 April 1791 but now lost. In A.M.'s thematic catalogue it was written as an
overture and chorus for a performance in a play by Sarti.

K616   ANDANTE FOR MECHANICAL ORGAN IN F MAJOR.   Written in
Vienna 4 May 1791. See also K608 (6).

K617   ADAGIO AND RONDO FOR GLASS HARMONICA IN C MINOR AND C
MAJOR.   Scored for glass harmonica: flute: oboe: viola: cello. Written in
Vienna 23 May 1791 for the blind pianoforte and harmonica player Marianne
Kirchgessner, who toured very successfully with this unique piece of music.
Also see K356 (12).

Extract letter 599, A.M. to C.M., Vienna, 11 June 1791:

"Dearest beloved. Cry out with me against every bad luck! Mlle Kirchgessner is not giving her class on Monday so I could have possessed you dearest for the whole of Sunday, but I will come to you on Wednesday."

K618   MOTET IN D MAJOR, *Ave Verum Corpus.*   Scored for choir: strings: organ. Written in Baden 17 June 1791, whilst C.M. was taking the waters in Baden, for the choir master of Baden Anton Stoll. The parish church in Baden had very limited resources and A.M. wrote this motet, "forty-six bars of sublimity", for strings and organ, which were available in the church.

Anton Stoll 1747–1805 was a schoolmaster, a music teacher and choir master in Baden and supplied C.M. with accommodation. He was given the original manuscript of *Ave Verum Corpus* which he later sold after A.M.'s death for a "large sum" (6).

Extract letter 595, A.M. to Stoll, Vienna, end of May 1791:

"Dear Old Stoll! Don't be a Poll! Will you please find a small apartment for my wife. She only needs two rooms, or one room and a dressing room. But the main thing is they should be on the ground floor ... my wife is coming to Baden on Saturday or by Monday at the latest ... if we cannot have these rooms, then you must look for something fairly near the baths: but the important thing is that they should be on the ground floor. This is the silliest letter that I have ever written in my life, but it is just the very thing for you Stoll."

K619   CANTATA, *The hour of the unfavourable.*   Scored for solo S with piano accompaniment. Written in Vienna July 1791, words by F.H. Ziegenhagen (8).

K620   THE MAGIC FLUTE, *Die Zauberflote.*   Zingspiel opera in two acts. Scored for 7 S (three treble): 2 A: 4 T: 5 B: chorus: 2 flute/piccolo: 2 oboe: 2 clarinet/basset horn: 2 bassoon: 2 horn: 2 trumpet: 3 trombone: timpani: glockenspiel: strings. Commissioned by Emanuel Schikaneder and words by him and A.M. from an original fairy story *Lulu* by Liebeskind, published in 1786. Written between June and 28 September 1791 and first performed on 30 September 1791 in Schikaneder's theatre, the Theater Auf der Wieden, Vienna, with A.M. conducting and Schikaneder as Papageno, and his oldest sister-in-law Josepha Weber-Hofer as Queen of Night and Franz Gerl as Sarastro (163).

An announcement for *The Magic Flute*:

> "A Grande Opera in two acts by Emmanuel Schikaneder, music by Herr
> Wolfgang Amade Mozart, Kapellmeister, actually in royal and imperial
> service, Vienna. Today Friday 30ᵗʰ September 1791 … have the honour to
> perform, and Herr Mozart, out of respect for a gracious and honourable
> public and from friendship of the author of this piece, will today direct the
> orchestra in person. The book of the opera, furnished with two cooper-
> plates, on which is engraved Herr Schikaneder in the costume he wears for
> the role of Papageno, may be had at the box office for 30 kr. The theatre
> painter Gayl flatters himself that he has worked with the utmost artistic
> zeal according to the prescribed plan of the piece. Prices for the admission
> are as usual, to begin at 7-o'clock."

The opera was from the beginning a "smash hit", the purse being shared on
an equal basis between A.M. and Schikaneder. It was performed 20 times in
October, and continuously in November and many times after A.M.'s death on
5 December 1791. Schikaneder went on to make a fortune out of *The Magic
Flute*, but did not give the due share of the purse to C.M. after A.M.'s death.

Zinzendorf's diary, 6 November 1791:

> "At half past 6-o'clock to Starkemberg's Theatre in the Vienna suburb … to
> hear the twenty-fourth performance of the *Zauberflote*, the music and the
> stage designs are pretty, the rest an incredible farce. A huge and at times
> uncontrolled audience."

A huge audience! By now A.M. really had a hit on his hands, as it played
nightly to packed houses; it attracted the "lower classes" who wanted an
opera as a cross between a pantomime, a Masonic ritual and a farce. Within a
month of this great success A.M. was dead.

Extract letter 599, A.M. to C.M., Vienna, 11 June 1791:

> "*I cannot tell you what I would not give to be with you at Baden instead of
> being stuck here. For sheer boredom, I composed today an aria for my opera
> [K620] I got up early at half past four … I am lunching today with
> Puchberg. I kiss you a thousand times and say with you in thought 'death
> and despair were his reward!',* [a quotation from *The Magic Flute*] *ever your
> loving and beloved husband W.A.M.*"

Extract letter 605, A.M. to C.M., Vienna, 2 July 1791:

> "*Please tell that idiotic fellow Sussmayr to send me back my first score of the
> first act, from the introduction to the finale so that I may orchestrate it. It*

would be a good thing if he could put it together today and dispatch it by the first coach tomorrow for I should then have it at noon."

Extract letter 611, A.M. to C.M., Vienna, 7 July 1791:

"... you cannot imagine how I have been aching for you all this time. I can't describe what I have been feeling – a kind of longing, which is never satisfied, which never ceases and which persists, nay, rather increases daily. When I think how merry we were together at Baden, like children, and what sad, weary hours I am spending here! Even my work gives me no pleasure strangely, because I am accustomed to stop working now and then and exchange a few words with you. Alas, this pleasure is no longer possible. If I go to the piano and sing something out of my opera, I have to stop at once, for this stirs my emotions too deeply. Basta. The very hour after I have finished this business I shall be off and away from here."

Extract letter 614, A.M. to C.M., Vienna, 7–8 October 1791:

"Dearest, most beloved little wife! I have this moment returned from the opera which was as full as ever. As usual the duet "Mann und Weib" and Papageno's glockenspeil in act one had to be repeated, and also the trio of the boys in act two. But what always gives me the greatest pleasure is the silent approval ... now for an account of my own doings. Immediately after your departure I played two games of billiards with that chap Herr von Mozart, the fellow who wrote the opera which is running at Schikaneder's theatre; then I sold my nag for fourteen ducats ... if I had nothing to do, I should have gone off at once to spend the week with you, but I have no facilities for working at Baden and I am now anxious as far as possible, to avoid all risk of further money difficulties. For the most pleasant thing of all is to have a mind at peace. To achieve this however, one must work hard, and I like hard work."

Extract letter 615, A.M. to C.M., Vienna, 8/9 October 1791:

"But Papageno's aria with the glockenspeil I went behind the scenes, as I felt a sort of impulse today to play myself. Well just for fun, at the point where Schikaneder has a pause, I played an arpeggio. He was startled, looked behind the wings and saw me When he had his next pause, I played no arpeggio. This time he stopped and refused to go on. I guessed what he was thinking and again played a chord. He then struck the glockenspiel and said in a loud voice 'shut up' whereupon everybody laughed! I am inclined to think that this joke taught many of the audience for the first time that Papageno does not play the instrument himself. By the way you have no idea

haw charming the music sounds from the box close to the orchestra – it sounds much better than from the gallery. As soon as you return, you must try this for yourself."

Extract letter 616, A.M. to C.M., Vienna, 14 October 1791 (this is the last letter A.M. wrote):

"Dearest, most beloved little wife. I called in the carriage for Salieri and Madame Cavalieri [his mistress] *and drove them to my box … they both said that it was an operone* [a grand opera] *worthy to be performed for the grandest festival and before the greatest monarch … Salieri listened and watched most attentively, and from the overture to the last chorus there was not a single number that did not call forth from him a bravo! or bello! It seems as if they could not thank me enough for my kindness … I hope that I shall certainly have a letter from you today, and that tomorrow I shall talk to you and embrace you with all my heart. Farewell, ever your Mozart."*

K621   LA CLEMENZA DI TITO, *The Clemency of Titus* (Roman Emperor 79–81AD).   Scored for 4 S: T: B: choir: 2 flute: 2 oboe: 2 clarinet/basset horn: 2 bassoon: 2 horn: 2 trumpet: timpani: strings. The play originally written by Metastasio in 1735 as a long three act somewhat tedious play. The court poet Caterino Mazzola "reduced the libretto to true opera". Commissioned by the Prague Impresario Guardasoni in July 1791 (A.M. still working on *The Magic Flute*), to celebrate the coronation of Leopold II (1791–1793). The time for working on this opera was so short that the recitatives were carried out by Sussmayr who also helped to fill in the bass. The admission was free for the first performance on the evening of the coronation, 6 September 1791, A.M. conducting (127).

A.M.'s thematic catalogue, 5 September 1791:

"… to be performed on 6th September, La Clemenza di Tito, *opera seria in two acts for the coronation of His Majesty Emperor Leopold II reduced to true opera by Sig. Mazzola, poet to His Serene Highness the Elector of Saxony – 24 numbers."*

From a Prague newspaper, 8 September:

"The day before yesterday in the evening there was a free opera performance in the National Theatre in the old town, which was filled largely by the high nobility, who are present here in great numbers. Their gracious Majesties arrived at 8-o'clock and were accompanied on their drive there and back by many thousand joyously cheering people."

Zinzendorf's diary, Prague, 6 September 1791:

> "... at 5-o'c to the theatre in the old town ... the court did not arrive until
> past 7.30 and we were regaled with the most tedious spectacle, *La
> Clemenza di Tito* ... La Marchetti sings very well, the Emperor is in
> raptures about her."

Extract letter 614, A.M. to C.M., Vienna, 7–8 October 1791:

> *... and the strangest thing of all is that on the very evening when my new
> opera was performed for the first time with such success* [The Magic Flute,
> 30 September] *Tito was given in Prague for the last time with tremendous
> applause. Cries of Bravo! were shouted as Stodla* [Anton Stadler] *from the
> par terre and even from the orchestra, what a miracle for bohemia but
> indeed I did my very best ... why, here is Don Primus with the cutlets! Now I
> am eating to your health it is just striking eleven. Perhaps you are already
> asleep! ST. ST. ST! I won't wake you ... 8 October. Do keep very warm so
> that you may not catch a cold. I hope that these baths will help you to keep
> well during the winter. For only the desire to see you in good health made
> me urge you to go to Baden. I knew I would feel lonely without you. I knew
> I should. Adieu, dear little wife. The coach is just going I trust that I shall
> have a letter from you today and in this sweet hope I kiss you a thousand
> times and am ever your loving husband W.A.M."*

K622 CLARINET CONCERTO IN A MAJOR.   Scored for solo clarinet: *age 35*
2 flute: 2 bassoon: 2 horn: strings. Written in Vienna in October 1791 for the
clarinettist Anton Stadler, part of the first movement already sketched out for
basset clarinet in K581 (27).

Extract letter 614, A.M. to C.M., Vienna, 7–8 October 1791:

> *"I told Joseph, to get Primus* [his servant] *to fetch me some black coffee, with
> which I smoked a splendid pipe of tobacco; and then I orchestrated almost
> the whole of Stadler's rondo. Meanwhile I have had a letter which Stadler
> has sent me from Prague – all the Duscheks are well ... they have all heard
> already about the splendid reception of my German opera* [The Magic
> Flute]. *"*

Haydn in a letter dated 13 October 1791, London:

> "My good wife wrote to me, and yet I cannot believe it, that Mozart was
> said to disparage me very much. [Haydn's wife Anna was much given to
> malicious gossip.] I forgive him for it; concerning the remuneration
> Mozart should go to Count Fries for information, with whom I have

deposited 500 ducats and with my Prince 1,000 gulden – in all well nigh 6,000fl; I thank my maker daily for this favour and I flatter myself I shall bring home another thousand in cash."

A.M. was seriously considering going to London, as Haydn had told him that he would be very welcome there and that he could make a lot of money.

K623 CANTATA, *Kleine Freimaurer-kantate.*   Scored for 2 T: B: flute: 2 oboe: 2 horn: strings. Written in Vienna 15 November 1791 and first performed on 18 November, A.M. conducting as his last public appearance. Masonic music for the new temple of the "New-Crowned Hope Lodge" (14).

K624 CADENZAS TWO PIANO CONCERTOS.   To be used in the first movement of subscription concerts that A.M. intended to arrange.

K625 COMICAL DUET, *Now, dear little wife.*   Scored for S: B: flute: 2 oboe: 2 bassoon: 2 horn: strings. Written in Vienna in August 1790 to be included in Schikaneder's play, *Der Stein der Weisen.*

K626 REQUIEM IN D MINOR.   Scored for solo S: A: T: B: choir: 2 basset horn: 2 bassoon: 2 trumpet: 3 trombone: timpani: strings: organ. Written in the summer and autumn of 1791 and was unfinished on A.M's death on 5 December 1791. Commissioned anonymously by Count Franz Walsegg-Stuppach, a fellow freemason, whose wife had recently died; he wished to pass off the requiem as his own composition. Completed after his death at C.M.'s request by Franz Susmayer. The first performance of the completed work was on 14 December 1793 in the parish church at Weiner Neustadt, the home of Count Walsegg (59).

In the summer of 1791 A.M. received a letter without a signature, requesting him to write a requiem, and to ask for it any amount that he wanted. As he was very much engaged in writing his last two operas it did not appeal to him, but as he needed the money he wrote back to say that he could not write it for less than 60 ducats, and not complete it until the winter of 1791. A servant came to A.M. and gave him 30 ducats and at his master's request said he would call again in three months and give another 30 ducats. A.M. started to write the requiem; *"I fear that I am writing my own requiem."*

A.M. became ill on 18 November 1791 and died on Monday 5 December 1791 at five minutes to one a.m. His final illness began with a swelling in the hands and feet with almost complete immobility. It was followed by vomiting and diagnosed as miliary fever, the cause of death being given in the register of death as heated miliary fever. The modern diagnosis is that the cause of death was rheumatic fever which led to kidney failure. There is no evidence to support the theory that he was poisoned by Salieri or anyone else.

Sophie Weber, C.M.'s sister, later wrote to Nissen, who was colleting material for his biography:

"Now I must tell you about Mozart's last days … how when Mozart fell ill, we both made him a night-jacket which he could put on, since on account of his swollen condition he was unable to turn in bed … I hurried along at fast as I could at Constance's request. Alas how frightened I was when my sister, who was almost despairing and yet trying to keep calm came out to me saying 'Thank God that you have come dear Sophie. Last night he was so ill that I thought he would not be alive this morning. Do stay with me today, for if he has another bad turn, he will pass away tonight. Go in to him for a little while and see how he is.' I tried to control myself and went to his bedside. He immediately called to me and said, 'Ah, dear Sophie. How glad I am that you have come. You must stay here tonight and see me die … I have already the taste of death on my tongue.' Sussamyr was at Mozart's bedside. The requiem lay on the quilt and Mozart was explaining to him how, in his opinion, he ought to finish it when he was gone. A long search was made for Doctor Closset who was found at the theatre … he came and ordered cold poultices to be placed on Mozart's burning head which, however, effected him to such an extent that he became unconscious and remained so until he died. His last movement was an attempt to express with his mouth the dream passages in the requiem. That I can still hear."

C.M. and her two children were granted a pension of 266 fl., one third of A.M.'s final salary.

From the register of deaths of St Stephen's Cathedral, Vienna:

"City number 970 Herr Wolfgang Amadeus Mozart, I & R Kapellmeister and Kammer Compositor, Catholic one male age 36 – sickness and manner of death severe miliary fever. Place and date of burial the 6th ditto the burial ground outside St Marx."

From 5 to 6 December the body was laid out in the house where he died. It was not a pauper's funeral but was the cheapest available. That neither C.M. or any close friends or freemasons attended the funeral is explained only by the simplicity that became customary for funerals at this time. Common graves were buried in three layers, and the fact that graves were not marked made it impossible later to identify with any certainty the place where he lay. General burial grounds were cleared every seven years.

Posthumous information

From the Vienna Zeitung, *7 December 1791:*

"In the night of the 4th and 5th of this month there died here the I & R Hofkammerkompositor Wolfgang Mozart. Known from his childhood as the processor of the finest musical talent in all Europe, through the fortunate development of his exceptional natural gifts and through persistent application he climbed the pinnacle of the greatest Masters; his works, loved and admired by all, bear witness to this and are the measure of the irreplaceable loss that the noble art of music has suffered by his death."

From a Vienna magazine, 9 December 1791:

"On the fifth of this month, in the early morning, there died Wolfgang Mozart, the I & R court composer. Famed throughout the whole of Europe at the early age of 35. Even the greatest masters were astonished at the rare talent of this great musician. But what has this richly endowed man left behind him? A name that will live for ever, but also a helpless widow with two orphan children and many debts."

A.M.'s debts at his death were approximately 3,000 gulden.

From a Vienna newspaper, 13 December 1791:

"Mozhart unfortunately had that indifference to his family circumstances which so often attaches to great minds. The widow of this man to whom so many crowned heads, to whom all Europe accorded un-stinted admiration; who, apart from his position as Hof-Kapells Meister, and deputy at St Stephen's had pupils taken exclusively from the highest and richest nobility; who could have, neigh should have, earned great riches for such famous works."

Invitation card from the Prague Theatre Orchestra:

"The Orchestra of the Prague National Theatre begs to announce that on the 14 December at 10-o'clock a Solemn Mass for Capellmeister and Kammercomponist Wolfgang Gottlieb Mozart, who fell peaceably asleep in

the Lord on 5 December in Vienna, will be held in the small side parish
church, St. Niclas as a mark of it's boundless veneration and esteem. To
which a very respectful invitation is extended to the high nobility and the
honoured public."

The congregation was enormous, as the whole church of St Niclas could
hold circa 4,000 people. "On the appointed day the bells of the church
were rung for half and hour; almost the entire city streamed thither,
so that the Walsche Platz could not hold any more coaches … solemn
silence lay all about, and a thousand tears flowed in poignant memory
of the artist who through his harmonies so often tuned all hearts to the
liveliest feelings."

Prague was once again showing its appreciation of A.M.

Haydn to a friend, 10 December 1791, from London:
"Like a child I long to be home again to embrace my good friends, only
regretting that I cannot do this to the great Mozart, if it is true – which I do
not wish – that he is dead. Posterity will not have such a talent again in
100 years."

A further obituary in a music magazine, 28 December 1791:
"It is our sad duty at the close of this year to impart to our readers an
intelligence which will cause great sorrow in the world of music, namely
that on the 5th day of this month the universally known, much sought after
and beloved Royal and Imperial Hofkammerkompositeur Hr. Mozart died
of a dropsy of the heart in his 34th year of his age. All Vienna and with the
Imperial city the entire musical world, laments the early loss of this
immortal man. His body has gone from us, his soul has soared upwards to
higher harmonies, and for our comfort and everlasting joy he leaves the
beautiful products of his mind."

From the Vienna Zeitung, *8 December 1791:*
"An inscription of Mozad's tomb.
He who lies here as a child added to the wonders of the world and as a
    man surpassed Orpheus with his playing.
Go on your way!
And pray for his soul!"

However no attempt was made at the time to identify the exact spot of A.M.'s burial and this epitaph was not used.

Haydn to Michael Puchberg, exact date unknown, London, January 1792:

"... I was beside myself for some considerable time because of his death and could not believe that Providence should so soon summon an irreplaceable man to the other world. Yet I regret only that he had not been able to convince the still unenlightened English of the truth of what I daily preached to them ... Dear friend, you will have the kindness to send me a list of the works which are not yet known here; I will spare myself no trouble to make them known for the benefit of his widow. I wrote to the poor lady three weeks ago myself, to tell her that when her favourite son is old enough, I will instruct him in composition to the best of my ability and without any fee, so as to some slight extent to take the place of his father."

The favourite son was Karl born 1784, who showed some musical ability and was educated in Prague and Milan. Haydn helped him in many ways and paid for some of his tuition.

Doctor Charles Burney wrote 'reminiscences' of A.M. which were eventually published in 1819:

"When Haydn was asked in our hearing by Broderip [Francis Broderip was a partner in the music publishing firm of Longman and Broderip in London] in his music shop, whether Mozart had left any MS compositions behind him that were worth purchasing, as his widow had offered his unedited papers at a high price to the principal publishers of music throughout Europe; Haydn eagerly said: 'purchase them by all means. He was truly a great musician. I have often been flattered by my friends with having some genius; but he was far superior to me.'"

At the time of A.M.'s death only about 150 of his 626 completed compositions had been published. C.M. found herself with an enormous number of manuscripts, from fully completed works to fragments and sketches. She asked Abbe Maximilian Stadler to help organise and evaluate the unprinted works, in order to sell them and assure herself some capital. With a complete catalogue then finished by Stadler, C.M. offered the entire collection for sale. Initially Breitkopf and Hartel expressed an interest and published a few but then backed out. Johann Anton Andre of Offenbach near Frankfurt had been told by Haydn that the manuscripts were available and after some negotiations with C.M. he purchased everything for 3,150 gulden.

The agreement between C.M. and Andre, 8 November 1799:

"Frau Mozart, widow, shall make over in to the possession of Herr Andre
those works of her deceased husband which are in her possession, and
marked with my, Andre's seal, consisting of fifteen packets, together with
the musical works specified and enclosed for the sum of Three Thousand,
One Hundred and Fifty Gulden, Vienna currency."

"Madame Mozart of Vienna, the composer's widow, has sold to me the
whole of the manuscripts of her husband that remained in her possession.
I am thus in a position to produce the most accurate edition of several
works of our beloved Mozart, both known and unknown."

Andre in his lifetime published around a quarter of the works that he had
bought, and it was not until 1875 that Breitkopf and Hartel, having purchased
from Andre's estate, finally published the definitive complete edition of A.M.'s
work. This edition used the Köchel numbering of 1862.

Masonic Oration on Mozart's death 1792:

"Allow me, my honoured and most worthy brethren to take advantage of
the present state of your minds; it has pleased the Eternal Architect to tear
one of our most beloved, one of our most meritorious members from our
brotherly chain ... Our worthy brother Mozart. Which of us would have
suspected the thread of his life to be so short? It is true, it is the sad lot of
mankind to have to leave behind an already distinguished career just as it
was coming to fruition."

A letter to N.M., early 1792, from a friend, remembering A.M. as a child:

"The son was three years old when the father began to instruct him. The
boy at once showed God given extraordinary talent. He often spent much
time at the clavier, picking out thirds, which he was always striking, and
his pleasure showed that to him it sounded good. The two Mozart parents
were in their day the handsomest couple in Salzburg. The son Wolfgang
was small, thin, pale in colour, and entirely lacking in any pretensions as
to bodily appearance. Apart from his music he was almost always a child
and thus he remained: and this is the main feature of his character on the
dark side; he always needed a father's, a mother's or some other guardian's
care. He could not manage his financial affairs, he married a girl quite
unsuited to him and against the will of his father and thus the great
domestic chaos at and after his death."

Count Waldstein to Beethoven, Bonn, 29 October 1792:
> "Dear Beethoven,
> You are now about to travel to Vienna to fulfil your wishes, so long
> opposed. Mozart's genius still mourns and laments the death of his charge.
> With the indefatigable Haydn he found refuge but not employment;
> through him he now wishes once more to be united with someone. By
> means of your ceaseless diligence you shall receive Mozart's spirit from
> Haydn's hands.
> Your true friend Waldstein."

From Madame Elizabeth Goethe to her son, Frankfurt, 9 November 1793:
> "There is no news here but that *die Zauberflote* has been given here
> eighteen times and that the house was always packed full. No person will
> have it said of him that he has not seen it, all the jobbing gardeners, indeed
> even all the inhabitants, whose children play the apes and lions, go to see
> it. A spectacle like this has never been known here before; the house has to
> be opened before 4 o'clock each time, and in spite of that some hundreds
> have to be turned away because they cannot get a seat – it has certainly
> brought the money in!"

She further writes to her son on 7 February 1794:
> "Just think! *Die Zauberflothe* was last week given for the twenty-fourth
> time with a tightly packed house and it has already brought in 22,000
> gulden! How was your performance of it?"

Johann von Goethe 1749–1832 was of course the famous poet.

From a music magazine, Chemnitz, 1794:
> "In this year nothing can or may be sung or played and nothing heard with
> approbation, but that it bears on it's brow the all-powerful and magic name
> of Mozart. Operas, symphonies, quartets, trios, duets, piano pieces, songs,
> even dances – must all be by Mozart, if they are to lay claim to general
> abbrobation. Sufficient to say that what is played or sung must be by
> Mozart and more particularly from his *Zauberflote.*"

From a music magazine published in London 1795:
> "... the applause which *die Zauberflote* received in Vienna was
> exceptionally great. It was performed sixty-two times in succession, and
> the attendance shows no sign of diminishing. In Vienna the curtain rises at

7-o'clock, yet for the first fortnight one had to claim one's seat as early as 5-o'clock, for a little later people were turned away in hundreds because the house was full. Only in the third week was it possible to struggle for and succeed in obtaining a seat as late as 6-o'clock."

Schikaneder was 'coining it in'; by rights 50 per cent of the purse should have been given to C.M., but he did not do so.

Announcement for an Opera by Mozart, Weimar, July 1795:
"Posterity does justice to the merits and genius of Mozart. His heavenly harmonies resound everywhere, on the stages of public theatres and in the salons of music lovers. Almost all of his greater and lesser works are already known either engraved or printed or in manuscript copies, and are to be found in the hands of everyone."

Goethe to Schiller, Weimar, 30 December 1797:
"The hope which you entertained for the opera you would have seen fulfilled to a high degree in *Don Juan* (*Don Giovanni*) however this piece too stands quite alone and all prospect of something similar has been frustrated by Mozart's death."

Goethe greatly regretted his failure to cultivate a friendship with A.M. as he wished his play *Faust* to be turned into an opera that could match *Don Giovanni*, but could not find a suitable composer.

On 8 September 1798 *La Clemenza di Tito* was given in the Freihaus Theatre, Vienna. In the programme for this concert, Schikaneder wrote:
"Mozart's work is beyond all praise. One feels only too keenly, on hearing this or any other of his music, what the Art has lost in him."

Nikolaus Nissen to Karl Mozart, Vienna, 13 June 1810:
"... you are aware that your great father left no fortune, only debts and an insignificant personal estate, which later yielded far less than was promised to your mother in the marriage contract. Since then it has been taxed and moreover it was left to your mother to determine and to place on deposit for her children a certain sum according to this settlement. This amount was 200 gulden each, for you and your brother."

Nissen had married Karl's mother (C.M.) in 1797; Karl was working as a teacher in Milan in 1810.

Hummel's sketch for a biography of Mozart being written by Nissen, circa 1825:

"… he was small of stature and of a rather pale complexion; his physiognomy had much that was pleasant and friendly combined with a rather melancholy graveness; his large blue eyes shone brightly, in the circle of his good friends, and he had many of them, he could grow quite merry, lively, witty even at times on certain subjects satirical."

Michael Kelly's reminiscences about A.M., London, 1826:

"I went on evening to a concert and was there introduced to that prodigy of genius – Mozart. He favoured the company by performing Fantasias and Capriccios on the piano-forte. His feeling and rapidity of his fingers, and the great execution and strength of his left hand particularly, and the apparent inspiration of his modulations, astounded me. After supper our host had a dance, and Mozart joined them. Madame Mozart told me that great as his genius was, he was an enthusiast in dancing, and often said that his taste lay in that art rather than in music. He was a remarkably small man, very thin and pale, with a perfusion of fine fair hair, of which he was rather vain. He was kind-hearted and always ready to oblige; but so very particular, when he played, that is the slightest noise were made, he instantly lay off."

Michael Kelly (1761–1826) was an Irish tenor who travelled extensively in Europe and became very friendly with A.M. and sang in the first production of *The Marriage of Figaro*.

From the travel diaries of Vincent and Mary Novello, Salzburg, 14 July 1829, on a visit to C.M. (now Nissen) and Wolfgang Mozart Junior:

"It is quite evident that Mozart killed himself with over exertion. He could never entirely abstract himself from his musical thoughts. Billiards he was very fond of, but he composed whilst he played, if he conversed with his friends, he was always at work in his mind. Necessity and the duties of his situation induced this habit which evidently wore out the system and would have produced death had he not been attacked with the fever which killed him suddenly … Madame confirmed the truth by sitting up all night with him whilst he wrote the overture to *Don Giovanni* He frequently sat up composing until 2 and then rose at 4, an exertion which assisted to destroy him."

A dinner conversation with Goethe, 3 February 1830:

"Dinner with Goethe. We spoke about Mozart. 'I saw him when he was a 7 year old boy' said Goethe, 'when he gave a concert on his way through. I myself was about 14 years old, and I can still quite clearly remember the little fellow with his wig and sword.'"

From the memoirs of Doctor Joseph Frank 1852:

"I found Mozart to be a little man with a broad head and fleshy hands; he received me rather coldly. 'Now', he said, 'play me something!' I played him a fantasia of his own composition. 'Not bad', he said, to my great astonishment. 'Now I'll play it for you.' What a wonder! The piano became a completely different instrument under his fingers. He had had it amplified by means of a second keyboard [see K467], which he used as a pedal ... 'I will play you another piece to you; you will derive more benefit from hearing me than from playing it yourself.' That is practically all I can remember having heard from this remarkable and great composer."

In the early nineteenth century Beethoven utterly dominated the music scene and had all but obliterated the appreciation of A.M.'s music. It was not until the early twentieth century that A.M.'s music came to be widely played. The advent of recording made his music widely circulated and today he is by far the most popular of classical music composers.

> *"When the angels sing for God they sing Bach*
> *and when they sing for pleasure they sing Mozart*
> *and God eavesdrops."* (Karl Bach) ? the musical family?